THE WAY OF THE HEART
∇

The Way of Heart

by
Raymund Andrea

AMORC

Published by the Grand Lodge of the
English Language Jurisdiction, AMORC, Inc.

Originally published as *The Andrea Lectures.*

© 1991 by Supreme Grand Lodge of AMORC, Inc.
All Rights Reserved

ISBN 0-912057-93-9

©1996, Supreme Grand Lodge of the Ancient & Mystical Order
Rosae Crucis
Published by the Grand Lodge of the English
Language Jurisdication, AMORC, Inc.

Cover Art: ©1996, Supreme Grand Lodge of the Ancient &
Mystical Order Rosae Crucis

Library of Congress Catalog Card No.: 96-068945

Revised Edition, 1996

10 9 8 7 6 5 4 3 2

Printed and Bound in U.S.A.

The Rosicrucian Library

Other volumes will be added from time to time.
Write for complete catalogue. See address on last page.

CONTENTS

Foreword

This special edition of the lectures of Raymund Andrea is a transcription of original Conclave lectures tape-recorded in Frater Andrea's home in Bristol, England, from 1954 to 1968 by Past Grand Master Robert E. Daniels and has been used by the Las Vegas Pronaos members as supplementary study material. Las Vegas Pronaos has generously donated this material to the Grand Lodge of the English Language Jurisdiction, AMORC, for the benefit of its members.

Frater Andrea said about himself, "You will find me in my books." Most students of the Order know him through his currently published works, *The Technique of the Master*, *The Technique of the Disciple*, and The *Mystic Path*. In reviewing *The Andrea Lectures*, the student will discover the practical, yet mystical, impact of Andrea's presentation and recognize him as an exponent of the highest ideals of the Rosicrucian Order.

Our Grand Lodge is pleased to share this generally unavailable work with students of mysticism and to contribute to the dissemination of the wisdom and practical insight of one of the greatest Rosicrucian philosophers, contemplatives, and mystics of our time.

Note: Several terms used by Raymund Andrea in his lectures may be unfamiliar to our readers. These include:

Grade   - now called Degree.

Manual   - a reference work formerly published by AMORC.

Rally   - now called Conclave.

HUMILITY

Lecture delivered 1954

O ur members will be familiar with the excellent Rosicrucian Code of Life, which is given in the Manual. It has a gravity and dignity all its own, and while some of its rules may be an ideal to be aimed at, rather than an easy daily achievement, yet to have the Code constantly in mind can only prove an inspiration and promote a silent molding of the character after the pattern of the master Rosicrucian. I want to quote one of these rules to you. It is simple, as all great utterances are, but of far-reaching importance. Here then is Rule No. 11* of the Code:

> *Flaunt not your attainments, nor boast of your Rosicrucian knowledge. You may be a Rosicrucian as a member of the brotherhood, but as a Rosicrucian in knowledge and power, the greatest and highest among us is but a child of the studies and unworthy of Rosicrucian recognition. Proclaim yourself, not as a Master, but as a Rosicrucian student and ever a student eternally.*

The teaching of this rule is clearly humility in the real sense, and here is an application of it. It would be a mistake, after having taken a few grades of our teachings, to set a price upon ourselves, because we are conscious of possessing a body of unusual instruction which seems to mark us out very definitely from those around us, whatever the personal value and attainments of the latter may be. We may find complacence in the thought that we now stand apart from others because we have embarked upon a course of esoteric training which promises initiation into knowledge and power which will confer upon us distinct advantages over our

---

*Note: In certain editions of the Manual this is listed as No. 10.

fellowmen. Yet nothing will so mark a man's inferiority rather than superiority in even entertaining this thought of an esoteric triumph over others.

The world is always with us, and we have much to do to adjust to it. But when we come into the Inner Place and look at ourselves from the standpoint of higher planes, humility is the only thing that profits us and helps us to see ourselves and others in a right perspective. And if there is anything that this particular rule I have quoted drives home, it is the unexpected conciseness with which it emphasizes the simple fact that, whether we are early in the grades or well advanced in them, we have nothing to boast of regarding the knowledge we have obtained through our study of them.

This rule demands much from us, more or less according to our temperament and particular mental background, but I think it will prove more searching to those in the early grades than to those in the advanced ones. For the assumption is that having, through several years of thought and meditation and active work and becoming assured of personal participation in the aura of the Order throughout the world, we shall share too in the mind and light of the master minds who inspire it, and that consciousness has its own power of silent enforcement of such a rule as this one. I do not say we cannot then make mistakes or fail of our ideals, but I do say we shall be acutely conscious of our mistakes and failures, and hasten to redeem them. I am sure that no member of sound mental development and wide sympathies would feel disposed, on reaching the deeply esoteric instruction, for instance, of the ninth grade to regard his standing in the knowledge of the Brotherhood as anything but a supreme personal test for its right usage and feel a special responsibility in his attitude towards others.

I feel, therefore, that this rule has special meaning for those in the earlier grades. Why? Because, for one thing, they had not yet been tried by the inner fire of ascension of consciousness. That is precisely why some in these grades have lost interest and fallen out. They were, after all, but on the neophyte path and so found, in their estimation, nothing very startling or profound in their studies. They had not yet passed more interior thresholds of instruction nor entered into their testing vibration. But those who have so passed some of these thresholds and awakened to wider vibrational areas of consciousness inevitably experience the reactions of that advancement. They are tried by fire.

What does that mean? It means that everything within the man is stimulated to increased tension. He brings himself unknowingly to his own trials, and if he has not that mental stability and sympathy I mentioned, then one of the first things he is prone to do is to sin against this rule. He will arrogate to himself knowledge and power which he does not possess and are far beyond his reach. The admiration and applause of others will mean far more to him than healing a bruised heart or a tormented mind.

I believe the reaction to that is swift and unrelenting, even if at the time invisible and unknown for the judge is the man himself, and he cannot escape his own sentence. So that, simple as this rule appears, there is underlying it, in respect for it, or in indifference to it, the hidden fire of esoteric teaching pointing to a student's ascension on the true path or his decline and fall from it. I do not speak of punishment, but there is far more sorrow resulting from one's conscious and willful failure in the things of the inner life than in one's failure to reach a goal in mundane things, for, in the one case, we betray the knowledge we have; in the other, circumstances quite beyond our control may have proved too difficult for us.

Now a word on a characteristic of the monographs you receive. There is one outstanding feature of the monographs which you cannot have overlooked. That is the opening Concurrences in them consisting of quotations from the works of famous thinkers of the past, not only those who were known as Rosicrucians, but all of them, men of profound thought and meditation, whose names are foremost in the world's literature as instructors and benefactors of their fellowmen.

The significance of this array of great names is that we recognize and acknowledge the world's great heritage of thought, that upon this platform of instruction and benefaction we stand side by side with those pioneers of many nations. We claim them as our own because we belong to them. We have the same ideals in view but with the added privilege of the deeper and more esoteric knowledge which has been vouchsafed to us from the secret archives of the Brotherhood. In these pregnant quotations we have a stream of potent thought, inspiration, and counsel calculated to actively stimulate our minds and inviting us to think empirically and so prepare ourselves for such mission in life as the cosmic powers may decree for us in this or in a future cycle, for the very essence of all our esoteric training in the grades is that of preparation. Remember the rule. We are ever students, which means now and in future cycles.

The very first quotation in the first mandamus monograph is a most apt one from Francis Bacon. It is, in a way, a comment upon the rule we have considered, for it shows how different students view their studies, their manner of approach to them, and how few hold fast to the highest purpose in them—which is to employ their enlightenment for the use and benefit of man. It reminds us of the rule, because the greatest error of many is to mistake the ultimate end of knowledge, and the rule admonishes us, not because we have little or much Rosicrucian knowledge to boast about it, as if we had attained, whereas compared with the masters of Rosicrucian science we are nothing but students.

The rule certainly does not flatter us, nor does the quotation, for the quotation reminds us of at least six kinds of students: respectively, those who seek the knowledge out of curiosity; those who seek it for mental entertainment; those who acquire it for the sake of reputation; those who grasp it for triumph in contention; others for money; and lastly, those whom the rule emphatically declares should seek it with humility, ever as students of the highest ideal and for the use and benefit of mankind.

It is in the last category that we should acknowledge ourselves to be. And to point the truth of this emphasis upon continuous studentship we have but to recall how little we know comparatively and how far short we come in our service to others or what we wish to do and achieve in the way of perfect counsel or in ameliorating opposing circumstance, but that is no reason for depreciating our present abilities and powers of execution in whatever direction they are enlisted. Rather, we should demand from ourselves the utmost possible from the knowledge we possess but without making any undue claims to others as to what we can achieve.

In fact, the basic law of our studies is involved here. We should deliberately bring ourselves to points of crisis on the path and cultivate climaxes of inner tension which will act as an evocative power upon the Inner Self and secure its response. If we do not demand much from ourselves, little will be given. This is only saying that we should try to rise to the occasion when the demand is put to us, and when once we are launched upon the path, we are all capable of more than we realize. A reserve of strength and wisdom has been accumulated and a response will come if we have confidence in it.

We may then perceive from these few thoughts upon merely one rule and one quotation from the work in our hands how much awaits our deepest reflection and use. The greatest thoughts are both hidden and revealed in the simplest and plainest language, and by applying our minds sincerely and humbly to the study of the monographs themselves, the wisdom of the Rosicrucian knowlege will be assimilated, and our studentship will prove a real preparation for association with the Master Minds of the Brotherhood.

THE WAY OF THE HEART

Lecture delivered 1955

To members in the advanced grades the names of several of the Masters will be familiar, among them that of the Master Moria. From what we have read about him he is a man of very striking appearance, of great personal power, with a style of utterance noted for its sententiousness, insight, and wisdom, and he is credited with the following cryptic words:

> *To behold with the eyes of the heart; to listen with the ears of the heart to the roar of the world; to peer into the future with the comprehension of the heart; to remember the cumulations of the past through the heart; thus must one impetuously advance upon the path of ascent.*

In my contact with members in the past, I have been acutely aware that the approach of some to their studies has been almost entirely a mental one. I know that individual temperament will strongly influence the kind of approach a student will make to his work. Some are almost entirely mental in approach while others are mainly emotional. The best results do not come from either the purely mental or an emotional attitude. Few combine both in a harmonious development, but no serious student will progress far on the Path without coming to realize that to be simply an introvert of the head is to close the door upon most valuable experience. If there is to be a balanced and useful development, he must also recognize the singular virtue in being an extrovert of the heart.

We have always thought of the Masters as being men of compassion. Indeed, they are often called the Masters of Compassion. This applies, of course, mainly to the Buddha and Christ, and as the Masters are acknowledged disciples of these two great ones, we cannot think of them other than men of compassion which means, that with all their extensive knowledge and wisdom, an all-inclusive love is also theirs. This is plainly evidenced in the first sentence of the quotation: *"To behold with the eyes of the heart."*

Now this is just what was not evident in some of the members I mentioned. They beheld truly with the eyes of the mind. They were very satisfied that they could see their way so clearly and rightly. They were focused on the mental plane, cold, detached, concentrated and that seemed to them all that was necessary. I have nothing to say against that except that they appeared to me to be looking away from Buddha and Christ: away from the Way of Compassion and feeling their sense of power and efficiency in trying to achieve personal supremacy in their own chosen direction. It is true that many go that way for years until life itself, under the increased tempo of their aspiration, teaches a sharp lesson; for life is very far from being an affair of the head only. Sooner or later, the heart of life demands recognition and, if it has been ignored, experiences painful and revealing will come and compel them to behold with the Eyes of the Heart. That is the first step towards a balanced development; and why should this not be so?

Soul culture, progress on the Path, the search after deeper knowledge and understanding of Self, does not fall within the same category as scientific, artistic, or literary research. This kind of research may be pursued without any thought or reference other than to personal culture and achievement. It is part and parcel of the ambitious life of millions of men aiming at legitimate success in the world, but mystical development is not the ambition of millions. It is the aim of the few and it has far more stringent rules to comply with! The first of which is equipment for personal and unique service to others. We cannot adequately serve others unless we behold them with the Eyes of the Heart. We shall never understand or help them truly if we are simply introverts of the head. The secrets of men are not in their heads but in their hearts, and it is there we have to look for them, feel them, and know them.

Now, the next statement in the quotation: *"listen with the ears of the heart to the roar of the world."* The roar of the world is continually in our ears. We are so accustomed to it that we take little notice of it. But to listen and try to interpret it with the Ears of the Heart opens a door to closer identification of ourselves with humanity!

What does the incessant clamor mean for the millions who participate in and cause it? What a contrast with the silent hour of meditation of the monk in his retreat, the mystic and the solitary in their hushed retirement. Karma conditions the one and the other, and while our special interest may naturally turn towards those who view the silence like ourselves, we need an inspired thinking and a live compassion for the multitudes who make our own lives possible in the midst of the turmoil. Do not overlook the concentrated toil, the burden of responsibility, the anxious efforts for adjustment of these multitudes who maintain the sound foundation and harmonious working of our so-called civilized life. Try to realize its manifold functioning and interpret it in the terms of the heart's stresses involved in it. We are a part of it—even when we try to avoid it—but the true mystic can never ignore it without deep loss to himself. In the words of the Scripture:

> *He dare not ignore the beauty and obscurity of those other Divine fragments which are struggling side by side with him and form the race to which he belongs.*

I need not say that the Mystic Way does not become easier through this willful descent into the heart and sensing life from that sensitive center. No indeed, rather it adds a burden to our journey! But if we have a call to the mystical life we must be ready to comply with the conditions of it. It is our own choice! Many on the Path have refused to accept this indication of the heart as their teacher. They have realized that to do so would stiffen the way of ascent. They have feared the penalties of increased sensitivity which they knew it would bring. Yet the Master has this sensitivity in perfection by virtue of accepting these conditions all along the Way, and it seems to me that if one really has a call to the Way he must discount the cost and be grateful for the rare opportunity of an incarnation.

These thoughts lead us to the next statement: *"to peer into the future with the comprehension of the heart."* This is a master thought and envisages a far reach of the Path. Only an illuminated heart can exercise that high prerogative, nor should we attempt to exercise it before the time! If we do, whether from ambition or presumption, we shall make mistakes and lead ourselves, and possibly others, astray. Even the culture of the heart for an incarnation may not confer this prerogative, and it is well that this may be so, for to see the evolving Karma awaiting us and others requires a balanced development of mind and heart which is all too rare on the Path.

How many of us, seeing the shadows on the Path ahead or the surrender of self to be demanded at a high portal, would yet go forward with inflexible will and purpose and not be checked by the voice of personality? It is amazing what some aspirants think they should be able to do after a few years of study of the Way! It was a failing of some highly intellectual men connected in the early years with the Theosophical movement in India. They demanded high privileges for which they were unready and instead of exercising a wise humility and patience—and being quite unprepared to peer into the future with the comprehension of the heart—they had recourse to spiritualism and the seance room, as if that byway of doubtful repute could make them as wise as their Masters!

"To remember the cumulations of the past through the heart." As first sight I thought we were on safer ground with this statement

than with that on the future, but clearly the reference here is to the Karma of former cycles—not merely the present one—and we see at once how very rare will be those who can review the broad sweep of past lives and see how they have fashioned the men they are. I know it is common enough for aspirants to feel pretty sure about their past incarnations, basing their conclusions upon certain features and attainments in their present cycle. I must confess that I have always been skeptical when meeting with those who have the greatest assurance about their storied past.

As in the case of peering into the future, I think alike well-balanced development is necessary in envisaging the past. There will be much awaiting the aspirant inscribed in that record of thought and action of past times and destined to come to fruition now and later which, if prematurely known, might destroy his peace of mind and the steadiness of his immediate progress. Here again, as regarding knowledge of the future, we may repose in the thought that the Cosmic Powers, to whom we look for guidance, will not lift the veil and reveal that which we have not won the right and strength to know and face with courage and compassion.

Why do I say compassion on coming to this, the final statement of the quotation: *"thus must one impetuously advance upon the path of ascent"?* Primarily because it points to what we need to culture for, in the immediate present. The word *impetuously* arrests my attention in the quotation. The towering presence and rather severe aspect of the Master "M" gives special significance to the word. Peremptory in speech and swift in action, the word *impetuously* suitably expresses his powerful will, but I would not use it as a word of guidance to aspirants generally. To advance impetuously, with a strong background of mature development, which knows itself, sees before and after, can stand against all odds, can rightly judge, thrust aside all obstacles and demand for itself the strongest discipline from life and Karma; surely this can only be a wise procedure for the very few. It would only be a fitting procedure for a close and accepted disciple of the Master, to whom the whole teaching in this quotation was familiar and practically demonstrable; for ourselves we shall be safer on humbler ground.

That is why I mention compassion; for there is an attainable stage of right development possible and needful for an aspirant when a deep and divine compassion pervades his attitude toward the world of human existence. It is not an easy attainment! The years must have taken their hard toll with him before the awakened heart comes to that point of long-range vision of lives, fighting for they scarcely know what, towards a goal they cannot see. The mind alone can never meet them face to face. It is far too circumscribed and unsympathetic.

If anyone thinks he will attain these graces of the inner man through logical exercise and mental acumen, the passing years will disillusion him. The heart, not the brain, is the center of life, and no matter how high he may have ascended in the realm of fact he will have to descend and wash his feet in the Blood of the Heart. That in itself will revolutionize his manner of approach to life, but he should now wait for this to be forced upon him, as it certainly will be if he petitions for advancement. He should try day by day to measure and judge all things and all people through the Fire of the Heart. He will only see things as they are, and evoke from others what is in them, by the magnetic radiation of the heart. According to the depths of experience we have sounded, through the awakened and compassionate heart, will be the response we shall obtain from those who have this latent experience in themselves and only need the right stimulus to express it.

I am saying nothing new! We know the books that make us think; the books that move and stimulate us belong to a different class. We know the people who make us think; how many do you know whose vibration kindles the Fire of the Heart and evokes the best we know in thought and action? I make this contrast designedly because we live in a scientific period, when science is reaching its high altitudes and its influence is worldwide. No matter what its value, in some respects its influence is a sinister one. The mind, not the heart, is in the ascendant and spirituality is at a discount—at a dead end. So true is this that the general public shows a profound fear at the advance of science. Not but far from it, is it showing a similar concern at the absence of interest in the life of a spiritual man. It is only concerned that the discoveries and exploits of the scientists shall not bring ruin and destruction upon its present way of life.

But the awakened and compassionate heart, to which the Master refers, is the offspring not of fear but of a spiritual consciousness which places its hope in an ascendancy to the high altitudes of the Spirit. And this is what we are pledged to, and whatever the future in the hands of science may bring, we must keep our eyes and ears intent upon the revelation which can come only from within. We must interrogate the heart in all things and use the mind to execute with understanding and compassion what the heart reveals. This is what the Master enjoins, and in trying to give it practical effect in our daily contact with others, we shall reach a point of attainment where we may safely, *impetuously,* advance on the Path of Ascent and our power of service will be vastly increased to the profit of many.

THE SECOND ADVENT OF CHRIST

Lecture delivered 1956

A second advent of Christ is a matter of special interest and much speculation among students of mysticism. The speculation concerns two different schools of thought. One school is a Western school which holds that the Christ will not appear again on the physical plane but only descend so far as the etheric or psychic plane. A contrary assertion seems to be that of an Eastern school of thought which maintains that the Christ will appear on the physical plane again among men at a propitious, but at present, a quite unascertainable epoch.

Obviously, declarations of this nature upon so momentous a matter would be expected to interest mystical students, especially when two schools of occult insight and authority are opposed as to the manner of the coming. What should be our attitude toward individual and independent declarations of this kind, while the truth of which we cannot possibly have any proof? Not one of criticism, I think, for they belong to the intangible, are beyond personal investigation, and clearly point to an event undoubtedly very far off in the future.

We are all familiar with the many findings and prophecies of science upon various matters which concern life on the material plane. We have seen and constantly see the objective realization of these prophecies. Many of them are startling and almost unbelievable when made but a few years ago. Then suddenly, when we had forgotten about them, a promised discovery has been made, a new power has been born, a fresh altitude has been achieved, and it becomes a fact or factor for use in daily life.

But we are upon different ground when declarations of the kind mentioned are made. This is far from being of the nature of a scientific procedure. We are not deeply skilled in the knowledge of futurity. There is no instrument in the hand of man whereby he can foresee and guarantee in time such a happening during a future evolution of humanity as the coming of an exalted being from high cosmic levels of spiritual existence. But as science can foreshadow the evolution of exceptional and unknown powers and processes through cooperation with the laws of nature, and we are now so accustomed to these eventuating within the limit of a few short years that we scarcely question any such prophecies, so it seems to me we should not dismiss occult declarations of a possible coming of Christ in a critical attitude or with emphatic disbelief, but regard the possibility with an open mind even though they differ as to the manner of His appearance.

Now the substance of these declarations about the second coming is that it will happen at some future time unspecified and unknown. But those who are conversant with mystical literature can point to instances of unquestionable veracity that the presence of Christ *now* has been a matter of personal experience and of psychic character. Those who have studied the life of St. Theresa, for example, will find therein several acknowledged visions which she had of the actual presence of Christ with her. She said that, on several occasions, she was granted a vision of Christ. In her own words, "For if what I see is an image, it is a living image, not a dead man but the living Christ." And she describes with such words as she can find the radiance which accompanied the visions. "It is not a radiance which dazzles, but a soft whiteness and an infused radiance which without wearying the eyes, causes them the greatest delight. Nor are they wearied by the brightness which they see, in seeing this divine beauty."

Or to take another instance nearer to our own time and a writer whose works are known to many of us; I refer to M.C., who wrote *Light on the Path* at the dictation of a Master and other inspired writings. In one of her books, she refers to a massacre of Jews in

Russia in 1905, when, in a vision of the Hall of Learning in which stood a great altar, the Christ stands on the altar steps, a superb figure of Light and Radiance, His hands uplifted in blessing the throngs of souls as they pass. Now and again, He draws one to him and presses it with a close embrace, removing from it by that contact all memory of the agony of its martyrdom.

These are testimonies of value and cannot be lightly dismissed. They point to a fact of psychic experience, vouchsafed in the one case to a saintly woman whose whole life was one long devotion to living the Christ's life and of inward conversation with Christ, and the other to a woman of well-known occult aspirations and who, in due course, was used by a Master to give to the world one of its most remarkable devotional manuals, *Light on the Path*.

There is no ground for doubting these testimonies. They are known to all classes of aspirants and accepted with reverence, and there are more testimonies of this nature which could be cited from other sources, so that the two declarations which I quoted of the two schools of thought, although of considerable interest, yet pointing as they do to a possible coming at some future time, which seem to be in a totally different category from these testimonies. For in these testimonies we have a kind of assurance that the coming of Christ is not a far-off divine event which may occur during this century or in some later one, dependent upon certain conditions of evolution of humanity as a whole, but that the Christ is here and now, a divine and guiding and helping presence and only awaiting recognition.

I recall that in the past there was some criticism here and there that our teachings made little mention of Christ. But what is the Rosicrucian science itself but a system of preparation to contact higher cosmic levels of consciousness which may at any time, in some particular cases, lead to the very presence of Christ on the etheric or psychic plane? What do our grades point to and gradually lead to but to an increasing inner perceptiveness and psychic contact with higher vibrational levels of cosmic existence?

The advanced grades seek to consummate the studies with a special technique whereby the initiate, contingent as always upon his individual permissive Karma, may bring himself within the sphere of the influence of the Masters of Compassion. And remember that the Masters themselves are known to be disciples of the Christ and sharing His life. Therefore, if we serve to the best of our knowledge to the end that we may be worthy of the special and individual guidance and inspiration of those masters who themselves serve the Christ, any criticism on this point may be discounted, for it reveals a lack of understanding and of our aim.

If, as one of these schools maintains, a great deal has necessarily to happen in the direction and quality of human evolution, but preparation in the direction of a larger and higher consciousness, before the Christ can appear and affect His mission in the world, then I think it is obvious that such a preparation will be of long duration. There are scant enough signs of His presence anywhere. Today, after the lapse of nearly a century, during which the Masters have been written and spoken of in occult and mystical circles, the subject is still far from one for general public proclamation, even among the intellectuals, and would obtain little credence if it were made so. Mystically and spiritually, we are on a pretty low scale of evolution.

On the other hand, if, as the other school maintains, the coming of Christ will be not on the physical plane but on the etheric level of consciousness, there is another opinion which may be considered as having weight and value. It is this: that the coming may well be, in a way, on the physical plane but through the medium of highly developed disciples of the Christ who will carry out His mission among men under His inspiration. I speak with no authority on this subject, but if contrary statements are made upon it in very emphatic terms, we have the right to consider both points of view and express an opinion about them. It is clear that both points of view cannot be accepted. One, that Christ will come again among men on the physical plane; the other, that He will never take again a human form or descend below the etheric level of consciousness. But whether we accept one or the other assertion, that does not alter in the least our aim in view of a coming of either description.

I fail to see how any of us aspiring to Master-contact cannot have constantly in mind the greatest of Cosmic Masters who functions at the highest point of evolution and whose influence is therefore transmitted from the secret place of the highest down to a wavering, suffering humanity. Moreover, in the Rosicrucian library, there are two remarkable volumes written by Dr. Spencer Lewis on the Master of Masters and His teachings. Therefore, for any one to ask us what we think of Christ and what place He has in our work is a plain confession of ignorance. If Christ traveled to the end of the Path, which embraces the whole of cosmic wisdom, and we are taking the first serious steps on that Path, we might ask what the critics know of this way and if they have taken any steps along it.

Indeed, this is the cardinal failing of exoteric Christianity today. It is proud of its confession of faith in the historical Jesus, but for profound belief in and acceptance of an esoteric Path leading to the vision of the living Christ, we have to look elsewhere. And it is just here that by focusing attention upon either of the two schools of thought mentioned as relating to a second coming of Christ that a result not fully anticipated may happen. It would tend to lead many to place their faith and hope in what such a coming would do for *them*, instead of thinking inwardly and seriously what they can and should do for themselves to be worthy of it and being ready to participate in it. To be deeply concerned or curiously interested about the coming of a world Master, yet do nothing in the way of self-study and preparation in order to recognize and be competent to assist Him in His mission to mankind should He come, is a poor substitute for discipleship. And I venture to say that this generation is unworthy of Him and would not recognize Him if He came. It is polarized in and hypnotized by objective life. It will pay any price for multiplying the fascinations and interests and rewards of that life.

Is it not then logical to conclude that if the Masters have thought it wise and necessary, for various reasons, to seclude themselves bodily from the hearts of men nor are likely to appear openly among men until much of the present world Karma has been liquidated? Far less likely is it, that the Christ, the greatest of Masters, will appear in any relatively near future to a world steeped in materialism which regards askance the comparatively few devoted to the mystical life and the discipline it entails. The chances are that, if not harried into exile, He would be hanged as a revolutionary and a nuisance and an avowed enemy to our much-vaunted way of life. This appeal to the future, this focusing of interest upon far-off and uncertain events to come, is distracting and unrewarding. There is enough before our eyes and our feet that warrants the interest of mind and hand. And this is where Rosicrucians have always firmly stood: in the present, facing the problems of the hour and endeavoring to the best of their knowledge and vision to show others something of the significance of the burden of the cross of life resting heavily upon them. But the lifting of that burden must be their own serious task.

So much of what is called the religious life is a form of escapism. It is an escape from self-discipline. Yet, without that discipline there is no progress on the Path of evolution, which is the purpose of our incarnation. So true is this that the Master, who inspired the works of M.C., stated bluntly that religion holds a man back from the Path. Only those who are on the Path will recognize and accept that simple but profound truth. The advancing soul has no need of church or creeds nor will ever be bound by them, because they are seen to be fetters and limitations, mental concepts, which imprison the spirit of man.

The purpose of the first advent of Christ was expressly to free the spirit of man through self-discipline to enter into the truth of the way. The church has not taught the esoteric way to Christhood. Creeds are merely a soothing substitute for it. And I believe that a second advent of Christ will prove to be far more dynamic and disrupting than the first. For we have reached a critical point in general evolution during the past hundred years, and such unusual powers are being scientifically developed through mental experiment and applied wholly to material ends, that the descent of an unprecedented stimulating energy, as may be expected to accompany a cosmic Christ, would shatter the idols and images which men worship and demonstrate full the supremacy of spiritual life.

A coming *today* may mean exile or death, but not *then*, for it is reasonable to think that the Christ would then have at His disposal the dynamic potency of a multitude of disciples who will have taken the stages of the Path, who will recognize the Christ and be pledged to fulfill His mission, and nothing will be able to withstand them. This thought is an encouraging and stimulating one. It gives abundant reason for us to persist on the Path we know, for the time will come when we shall be called to direct cooperation with the cosmic intention. And everything we have endured and suffered will be forgotten in the mastery we shall be able to offer in the fulfillment of that intention.

THE HONORABLE SKEPTICS

Lecture delivered 1957

M any who have written hard things about the drift in our national life since the war have been thought unduly pessimistic by those who have chosen to shut their eyes to it. But shutting one's eyes to facts, which responsible writers and critics have not hesitated again and again to declare in no uncertain terms, does not obliterate the facts. They are far too widely known to be ignored or forgotten.

Recently, a former headmaster of a school in Scotland had this to say: "A sick civilization is throwing up five types of young people—the lawless, the listless, the pleasure and sensation addicts, the angry young men, and the honorable skeptics." No one appeared to have contradicted or questioned the statement. The majority of those who read it would presumably have shrugged their shoulders and turned quickly to more exciting or comforting news. But the statement was a grave indictment of a large section of our boasted civilization. The prevalence of the well-marked first four types, no impartial observer could deny. So prevalent are they that no decent individual can very well avoid them, and if he could he would still be more or less subject to their degrading influence.

But I was chiefly interested in the fifth type, the honorable skeptics. Whether the term "honorable" was used ironically or in appreciation of the type, I cannot say. Persons who are honorable we usually respect because they have commendable qualities and are of good report. One writer has said that the avowed skeptic is only sure of uncertainties. Well, if the skeptic declares openly that this or that philosophy or belief leaves him uncertain, affords no foundation to build on, there is more hope for him in the future than for either of the other mentioned types. It is not a crime or a defect of character that an individual is a skeptic. Some of the great characters in the world's literature have been declared skeptics. They have been thinkers of deep understanding and extensive knowledge and have plumbed the depths of more philosophy and science than we can boast of.

I recall that a well-known mystic, in some of his fantasies on Karmic Law, pointed the curious fact that some of these famous characters and writers had spent nearly the whole of their lives in advocating this or that philosophy or system of belief, and spent their latest years in repudiating all they had hitherto believed and promulgated. The apparent reason for this was, according to him, that some phase of Karma, hidden up to that time, suddenly emerged into consciousness from the past and swept them helplessly into a current of belief, or non-belief, directly opposed to that which they had formerly held and upon which their reputation was founded. No doubt they were considered thereafter as avowed skeptics, but they were honorable ones. However, these were skeptics at the top, and we are thinking now of a different type at the bottom.

Now the headmaster of the famous school, in his summary analysis of our sick civilization, had not only weighed up our society very astutely but would also have had ample opportunity of observing these types during his professional life, for it is common knowledge that there is a strong current of skepticism running in school and university student life today. The orthodox religious teaching which obtains in practically all of the educational institutions, whether professed by many or few, has, to a great extent, lost its influence in student life. It is not that these skeptics are ignorant of the philosophies and general beliefs of traditional systems of thought. It may well be quite the reverse, for the really promising individuals among them have well-digested knowledge of these and find them completely unsatisfying and leading to no certainty of fullness of life or incentive to worthwhile action. They have reached their decision honorably during their most promising years and ended in a philosophy of their own: a philosophy of doubt.

It may be said that this is no business of ours, but a Rosicrucian cannot adopt that attitude. We should not be ignorant or turn aside from anything which so deeply lowers the standard of the social order. We should study and understand it and observe where we ourselves stand in relation to it. We know that the Rosicrucian teachings, for instance, have profound meaning and an undecaying foundation. Skeptics young or old may, if their mind extends its investigation so far, regard it offhand as just one of the innumerable branches of magical and supernatural belief which periodically descend upon us from afar, flourish for a day, and are forgotten.

We, like others, have failed to reach the younger generation in its student life. We have not found an effective way of approach to it. Moreover, the confirmed skeptic can be a formidable influence in his own opinion, no matter how misguided we may think him to be. He will not condescend to change his opinions or swerve from his path and voluntarily come to us. An approach has to be made to him with so strong an appeal that his armor of doubt shall be penetrated and lose its deceptive invulnerability. No ordinary method of approach will do this. This is far from being an indictment of ourselves. Nobody else either has found a way or approach to it, neither society, cult, movement, or institution. The responsible agent is evolution itself which brooks no interference with its august laws. Whether this is a progressive or regressive evolution has been much a matter of speculation. We are too involved and submerged in it to take a detached and unbiased view of it.

The young skeptic then is declared to be one of the conspicuous ingredients of our notorious sick civilization. Church and dogmata leave him cold. The idealists, straining after their utopias, are regarded with like contempt. The philosophers, speculating through the centuries upon the inscrutable universe, contradicting one another and hovering on the confines of skepticism themselves, these are merely a mental gymnastic for him. As for the supernaturalists and spiritualists, none so doubtful as they, and peculiarly an object of derision. Therefore, the mental outlook of a skeptic, if a pathetic one, is also a very interesting one.

As for the other four mentioned types, many will consider them as beyond redemption. It certainly would require much to redeem them. Perhaps more experience of life and personal suffering will do much in time. Suffering they will sometime have to face, whether physical or mental or both, because the term of life set for us here demands it. Whatever our belief or non-belief, our destiny being bound up with the destiny of the world, suffering is and will be the compelling influence in human life on its way to inner awakening and spiritual vision, and it will be these four types who will have the hardest lessons to learn. There is no escape in caring for nothing but regarding life as a lighthearted adventure, nor is there any escape for the skeptic at the other end of the scale. Knowledgeable and commendable in character as he may well be, he will feel the pressure of life in a more acute degree. He will experience an uninspiring inner vacuity, a persisting frustration of mind and consciousness of being outside the precincts of an assurance of soul and spiritual guidance which are an ever-present solace and directive in the lives of their wiser fellowmen.

It is well to be cognizant of these phases of racial evolution in the midst of which we live. I know very well that we are practically helpless to change them. We are well aware that, as barrier after barrier between the various classes are falling away under the impetus of evolutionary trends, the skeptic becomes more and more in evidence and in increasing number. Moreover, this skepticism affects in subtle ways the social life. Ostensibly, we may ignore it, but actually the influence of this thought form materializing a philosophy of doubt is an unseen obstacle in the path of our own aspiration and development.

In the closing of the ranks of humanity, it cannot be isolated in a department of influence of its own, detrimental to and recoiling only upon itself. Like other thought forms, it has attractive power and draws weaker minds into its orbit. It has a group power which is not in harmony with cosmic law but in opposition to it, and the man who ignores that law or willfully opposes its good intention stultifies his soul life and invites forms of suffering decreed for his redemption.

The fact that we are helpless in the face of these evolutionary abnormalities, which are a menace to higher and spiritual culture, is the strongest reason for observing, understanding, and criticizing them. If our civilization is sick, we as Rosicrucians should be the first to realize it through psychometric sensitiveness, and long before it is professionally indicated to us, we should have sensed it, interrogated and discussed it, and be well posted as to what is causing its sickness. The early Rosicrucians did not have to be informed of the evils of their time. They were the first to detect them through their science and expose them, and they were the first to be damned for doing so. In their time the Rosicrucian Path was a trial of fire, a path of scorching revelation with persecution on each side of it. Where is that path today?

It should be indicated to those outside our ranks that we are not so occupied in saving our own souls that we shut our eyes to what actually is outside and pass by the skeptic on the other side as if he never existed. He confronts us oftener than we think and we should at least confront him with new enlightenment which may induce him to reflect more seriously and endeavor to view his life in a different light and banish the philosophies and beliefs which have really failed him. We must assure ourselves that skepticism does not mean ignorance. It often means that the influence of a scientific and intellectual trend of our time has captured the imagination and submerged all interest in the possibility of contact with the higher levels or consciousness, and any tendency on our part to regard the skeptic or any other thinker as unworthy or inferior because of contrast with our particular way of life would prove conclusively that the imperishable wisdom of Christ and Buddha, and every other illuminist who has gone before us and far beyond us, has lost its true significance for us.

However irrelevant this particular theme may appear to be, it has a value in focusing attention upon one of the signs of the times. There is a challenge in it, however little we can do objectively about it. We know the value of concentrated thought force upon any specific subject in any particular direction, and we can add to the potency of the Rosicrucian thought form we have created through the years and thereby increase its attractive power in many mysterious and unknown ways. It can open many closed doors and impart a new impulse to many a closed mind quite beyond our conscious knowledge. That is the only assurance we have in the Order in facing problems of others outside in the world as large. What cannot be effected directly and with sure results we may help to be done from the cosmic level from which the forces of good operate and whose one purpose is to assist the upward evolution of man.

Our thought, therefore, of the skepticism of our time leads us back to the thought of the value of our own studies and can promote a new resolve to make them more effective. Our purpose is not simply to repeat the work and attainment of a past year but rather to feel certain dissatisfaction with what has been achieved, inciting to fresh ideas and methods of research and application and drawing forth still latent abilities in the older members and inspiring the younger ones to a deeper sense of responsibility in sharing in this united effort and, in conclusion, never forgetting that in thought and meditation, regarding our own inner develop-

THE WAY OF THE HEART

ment with all seriousness, and only so, can we register definite advancement from year to year.

I lay stress upon this because some who will come to us in the near future will belong to a sixth type not mentioned. They will not be lawless, or listless, nor pleasure addicts, or angry young men, or even skeptics. They will be tinged with a common disease of the age: An easy way to obtain much in a short time. Even the skeptic will be more preferable than these, if he has studied and challenged and found no solution to his perplexities and if he has sharpened his mind through thinking and meditation. So much the more should we, through thought and meditation, be skillful in sounding the basic tones of the deeper life and be able to meet the challenge of any type.

THE ESOTERIC ASPECT
OF CHAPTERS

Lecture delivered 1958

We are proud of the Francis Bacon Chapter and for good reason. It has been our privilege to form it, nourish and build it up, in one of the most difficult and testing times imaginable from every point of view. The war scattered our members abroad and checked their activities for cooperative endeavor, but it did not destroy our purpose and resolve. In 1947, a few enthusiastic members associated with Frater Lake, and the chapter was inaugurated. The progress it has made since then you know, and highest praise is due to those who have brought it to its present influential standing.

I want to refer now to a more esoteric aspect of chapter or group life. I suggest that sincere and dedicated work in the Chapter, when once a steadfast rhythm of activity has been set up among its members, should attract within its sphere hierarchical power hitherto uncontacted. Its purpose is not being fulfilled simply by periodical meetings together of its members. Something living and dynamic should come to life within it as an anticipated result of the united mental, emotional, and spiritual aspiration of its units.

I have often referred to the rhythm it is desirable to establish within a group. This is particularly a musical term, but it is also applicable to written and spoken language and to action. In a Chapter it should be seen and felt in a certain measured, harmonious, and balanced expression on the physical, emotional, and mental planes towards attunement with the inner spiritual self. There is only one way to this and that is through ever deeper knowledge of oneself and no less of those with whom we have to work out our destiny in this cycle.

Now one of the outstanding characteristics of Chapter life should consist in a deliberate elimination of individual purpose in the interest of the group organism. I know that all will not be ready for this step of preparedness, for it entails and demands far more than appears at first sight. It may be asking too much of the younger aspirant. Nevertheless, it can be said as an example, and for encouragement, that the more advanced ones do not feel it a hardship nor a great self-sacrifice nor have they a feeling of personal loss in this matter of adjustment. Quite the contrary— and in fact in real inner development, it should lie far behind us, and where this is so, we may be sure that the peculiar fire of long probation has eliminated any counting of the cost in a worldly sense.

To work efficiently in a corporate capacity demands a certain degree of self-effacement. To work under stipulated conditions for mastership in the future is not an easy role for the personality. Some meet here their greatest difficulty, but once a powerful harmonious rhythm is felt with in the group, its influence will be effective in helping the less advanced to align themselves with it, but there must be a central rhythmic radiation among its chief members, to provide the necessary and stable stimulus. Sometimes personal factors have been strongly in evidence on entering a Chapter, but under the searching vibration therein, the guidance of instruction given and the dominant tone of the group as a whole, these hindering factors gradually lose ground, and an alignment of purpose is achieved.

Corporate group life always demands readjustment. Personal activities have to be subordinated to the life of the group soul. This does not call for any killing of the ambitious life of the mind. The ambitious mind is an asset and becomes of greater use when the strain and stress of desiring to express only individually is transmuted into the inclusive expression of the group.

I am looking at our Chapter life from quite a serious angle. For the individual member, it has an element of paradox in it. We want him to be expressive to the fullest degree but for the group, not for himself, and this means, that in some respects, he will have to stop short of some things he could do or would have done and become quiescent and subject to the group purpose.

In group functioning these individual adjustments will have to be made even if sometimes not altogether acceptable. A group of intellectuals assembled for concerted action would undoubtedly require some modification of individual views, some relinquishment of opinions, possibly acceptance of unfamiliar conditions by its units in order to ensure the effectiveness of its united action. The reasonableness of this is not questioned. All the lines are drawn in, tensed or relaxed, and ultimately adjusted towards one center of clear knowledge and procedure.

I submit that the same process should not be questioned in the life of a Chapter. For no matter what a member may feel about himself in his private life and sanctum, what opinion he may have of himself and his knowledge, when he comes to associate with his fellow aspirants in the name of advancement and service, he must be prepared to modify that assessment, not to assert, but to adjust himself to the larger group purpose. All the groups, whatever their character, undergo periods of happy adjustment and of temporary maladjustment. Both should be accepted with equanimity and an understanding that lessons are being learned and assimilated and valuable experience gained as in no other way. The influence of the center will reach the periphery. The important thing is that the central radiation of the group should be strong, steady, and exemplary.

I said that a member should be prepared to modify his assessment of himself when he enters upon Chapter life. I have in mind one particular modification. A member may be presumably acquainted with many schools of thought and practice, but in his Chapter life what he has assimilated from those sources should not be ostensively asserted but kept in abeyance. Let them influence his private way of life as they will, for good. In the Chapter, he is not an exponent of theosophy or anthroposophy or Buddhism. He is a student of Rosicrucianism with well-defined lines of thought and action to be considered and used.

Prior to entering upon group work, the aspirant pursues more or less a strictly individual path of development under the guidance of miscellaneous instruction he may have contacted. There has hitherto been no necessity for the more impersonal procedure which a group demands. It is sufficient if he brings into it the mature results of his studies in the nature of an organized mental and emotional life directed to useful service. He should not feel that he has authority to impose any extraneous views absorbed from those studies upon the instruction and procedure of the Chapter.

I will quote from a letter I received from a member which bears precisely upon this subject. He says that he esteems highly Eastern writings and teachings, but it is the undue emphasis on them which is distressing since it produces in some male students, in particular, an esoteric mental hypnosis which is dangerous both to themselves and Rosicrucianism and renders a Convocation little better than a pharisaical farce. Those are strong words from a group member but not from the Francis Bacon Chapter. They illustrate what I am suggesting that a member should avoid. It is obvious that he is a Rosicrucian student or he would not be in the Chapter at all, and his aim should be to incorporate himself into its life and purpose. The central and established rhythm of the Chapter cannot be expected to alter its tempo and accommodate itself to any imperfect or challenging rhythm in its units. It is they who must exercise acquiescence, a receptivity and understanding of what the Chapter provides for them. For if they elect to hold fast to their own views and procedures, corporate action is at an end. They remain valuable units still, within their own individual spheres, but so far as they are concerned, there is no real co-partnership with the group.

I have no wish to depreciate any of the systems of thought mentioned. I am not discrediting them in the eyes of any student. I only say they do not belong to the Chapter, and the quotation I have given plainly shows the possible disharmony and just criticism likely to ensue if they are brought in. It is not well to emphasize the possibility of negative results in group combinations. They are mentioned rather to strengthen the resolve of those who participate in them to spare no effort in preparing themselves to accept the conditions, at their own free will, which must be imposed by authority upon the behavior within them.

If some negative results are sometimes recorded, it does not indicate want of insight on the part of those responsible for the election of units in a group. It is a case of material, suitable and valuable in many respects, being given an opportunity to prove itself under discipline with every assistance to ensure success but sometimes failing temporally to carry the tension involved in it. Many who come in are actuated by a spirit of service; others just as surely look for special privileges from Master contact. While the few are not concerned about the immediate rewards of service, the many look for these rewards from the beginning. Those who are esoterically ready experience no surprise at the declaration that the emphasis in this work is shifted abruptly from individual to group importance.

Nevertheless, it is the greatest test that can be conceived of true impersonality in an aspirant and therefore not surprising if some should retreat even after acceptance of the conditions imposed upon them, for modern life has stressed the importance of personality and individual power beyond anything hitherto known, and a sensitive aspirant is sometimes swept into the vortex of this compelling influence to an extent he is not fully conscious of. Yet the personality, so pathetically strong to hold its own because of the pressure of the demands of everyday life and circumstance, must lose ground when it passes within the group rhythm.

It is in this connection that some who were promising individuals in the past have failed. They have failed in all kinds of groups, for the increased power which comes to an aspirant under group discipline is sometimes a direct challenge to him to misuse it or to hold it exclusively or chiefly for personal achievement. There is nothing in the personality itself which will give immunity from this challenge—on the contrary, its nature is to foster it. It has the strongest incentive to seek and use power to the limit for its own interests. The only inhibition against this arises at the central heart of the aspirant's inward life. It does not come from the ordinary moral code of right and wrong, nor from the aloofness of intellectual integrity, nor yet from a cowardly fear of losing prestige in the eye of authority. It is a fiat of the soul's spiral of attainment before the Master has called it to share the grace of His presence.

Indeed, this discipline within the group has a value in preparation which complements the instruction he receives in it. If approached in all seriousness and with understanding, he can help to fashion an instrument for the Master's use when He elects to call an initiate for special service. Hence the necessity for a wholehearted acceptance of the unique opportunity of Chapter affiliation from a clear mental appreciation of the demands which it must enjoin and an anticipation of the opposing individual factors which this group combination will inevitably disclose and his insight must reconcile.

It is much if an aspirant has through the years learned, in spirit and in truth, the nobility and beauty of self-effacement. It cannot be taught. Even occultism can fail to instill it into the heart. It flowers from a kind of maturity in the man himself, after long and patient vigils of many kinds. It is really life having been lived deeply, through the incarnations, an ever-present consciousness of what life means to striving and worthy souls. They can be seen here and there along the paths of life and endeavor, men who have passed their treasures of thought into the stream of time without recognition and never seeking it. They recognize a power within them not their own which must be given back to the world in forms of beauty and utility to ennoble and educate whomsoever they will. And what is worthy of note for us in this characteristic of the true creator and server is his complete dedication and abdication, the divine necessity which constrains him to give himself, in disregard of all personal considerations.

It is something akin to this that I have in mind when I refer to the esoteric aspect of Chapter life, that it should attract within its sphere hierarchical power hitherto uncontacted. The aspirant should cultivate a sensitivity to what the combined group power to which he has access can produce within him.

And if I may conclude upon a high point for consideration, I would say this: we are qualifying for Master recognition and cooperation, and we should know that we cannot expect to have that intimate association until we comply with the terms which it demands of us. The corporate life of a Chapter can provide a vehicle for the manifestation of cosmic forces and direction, which will make that association possible, but only after the voices of self have passed into the silence.

THE WORDS OF A MASTER

Lecture delivered 1959

I begin with the words of a Master:

> *Does a man know when he performs his best action? What person can tell which of his words has had the most influence? What person can tell which of his thoughts has reached the highest sphere? Perhaps such knowledge would cut down the striving toward development for it might stir up pride. Thought sometimes actually reaches the higher spheres and remains near the altar.*

I think these words carry a message to us of great encouragement. I am sure judgment of ourselves in daily contact and especially in our Chapter work is far from justified. I know I have suggested a high ideal for ourselves in our work, but we should not overlook the fact that an ideal of that nature is what we envisaged, a condition of realized attunement to be hoped for, not to be expected to be attained forthwith. I do not say this in a derogatory sense, as if too much cannot be expected of us, but with the thought in mind that fulfillments on the Path are slow and halting within our conception of time. How would they be regarded within the timeless conception of the Cosmic? The answer appears to be suggested in the quotation.

A research study in a Chapter was referred to as a small effort of the member who made it. But a small effort can be quite original and very interesting and inspiring to many. We are so bogged down by life around us, with conceptions of right and wrong, good and ill, values and non-values, labeled and accepted by the senses and the mind as a standard of judgment for all things, that the high and clear insight of the soul does not get a chance to reveal the silent truth shining beyond them.

There is a divinity within us, but we are human beings with a peculiar weight of Karma or past history which is constantly urging us to adjust to the present time. That is a fact of much importance and the circumstances of each of us should incline us to consider it seriously and observe what it means to us. We often refer much too freely to Karma as a term which defines the general trend of life, but we forget that it has fashioned us down to our fingertips and cast the lines for tomorrow. How much good comes to us without our asking or expecting it and how much towards our path just as unexpectedly and unwished for and for which we see no justification?

This two-way activity is very noticeable in the lives of aspirants, no less so, often much more so, than in the lives of those who take no thought for higher culture. Without this acceptance of the hidden side of life, of the past working into the present, life would be an incomprehensible puzzle, as it actually *is* to millions of our fellow beings. One wonders sometimes how, without a stable assurance and understanding of the facts of our incarnation, they maintain a grip upon existence at all. I think they survive mainly through the common humanity and help of those around them until at some point, through the reacting urge and discipline of the cycles, they are brought to seek the deeper truths of life and ultimately find themselves upon the first stages of the Way. Life without fails them and they are driven inward. This would appear to be happening at the present point of history to an unprecedented degree. We do not, nor shall we, observe large sections of society accepting offhand the truths of the Path—the facts, for instance, of Karma and reincarnation.

But what we *do* observe is that because of the swift and startling advance of scientific discovery and what it is likely to entail in the near future, together with the keen desire for knowledge of all kinds of culture on the part of increasing numbers, especially among many in their early years, and further, and more vitally important than anything else, the quickening pulse, shall we say, of hierarchical intention in the evolution of the races. The ground is being rapidly prepared for the advent of greater souls of high caliber who will demonstrate the truth of the Path in a way which will compel attention. And observe this: if the pulse of evolution of the general mind is being pushed rapidly forward to wider understanding and more inclusive purposes, we may be certain that the cosmic pulse is accelerating also and causing it, and what we sense is the decree and outworking of cosmic purpose.

We ourselves, in our Rosicrucian studies, are witnesses to this purpose and are doing what we can to give greater effect to it. The visible results may be scarcely noticeable in the busy life around us, but it is esoterically aligned with the cosmic purpose, and later on we shall better judge the value of it. Generally speaking, interest and attainment in the esoteric realm are little in evidence today, but the Masters exist; they know their plan; they discern the trend of events, and if the nations are still at cross purposes with one another over their rights and wishes, in world conquest, and even where they are not, it shows scant interest in the culture of the higher faculties of man, or even do not believe in their existence, dedicated in the main as they are to sensuous attractions and a competitive race for mental domination and the conquest of physical space. Nevertheless, the Masters' plan is not thereby thwarted.

If it is said that the trend of world events could be a part of the plan—in other words, what is must be and all is well—then there is nothing the individual can do about it. I incline to a different view. The nations can be so unspiritual and therefore shortsighted as to think that their own little plan—the plan of politicians, statesmen, scientists—is the answer to all problems and difficulties. Leaving aside the politicians and statesmen, who moreover can be proved so often far less well informed than the people for whom they legislate, consider science. Science, which can be so valuable, has nevertheless cast over humanity an atmosphere of fear, anxiety, and distrust. I think that is diametrically opposed to the Masters' plan for humanity which legislates for universal love, individual security, and perfect trust.

It also may be said that the words of a Master, for instance, written over fifty years ago have no application today. Indeed? Listen to them: "The moral and spiritual sufferings of the world are more important and need help and cure, more than science needs aid from us in any field of discovery." I do not think Masters make mistakes when they make prophetic statements of that nature. These words are prophetic and they are more pertinent today than when they were written. For if all the so-called leaders of humanity and rocket-minded scientists focused their energies in a combined effort upon lifting the moral and spiritual sufferings of the world—infinitely greater as they are through a marked decline during the present century—the plan of the Masters would stand revealed, known and brought to fulfillment, because they would then be worthy of it, but the plan waits. The nations have bypassed it, thinking—if they think about it at all—that the plan of a Christ and His Masters is worthy to take its place among the hallucinations of a Swedenborg, to whom the presence of Christ and the spiritual world were as familiar as the world around him.

Looking at the world picture in all its somber colors, we have a duty not to be discouraged by it. For the more bewildering and threatening it may appear, the more certain we are that what little we can do is needed in it. We find ourselves karmically implicated in the midst of increasing problems of states and individuals. They do not grow less. They multiply with the years because the *mind* of man is in the ascendant instead of the *spirit* of man. All the more determined should we be not to be diverted from our aim and purpose. This is our Karma, here and now, written within and before us and demanding attention and interpretation. Without being unduly introspective, we turn the searchlight upon ourselves, patiently and without bias, being under no illusion as to what we are, what we believe, and what we can do. It is not an easy task nor can it be a swift one. A quiet searching of the heart and mind in prescribed moments is far from being a selfish occupation. It is imperative on the Path, and the quotation I gave was to encourage us in it. When we think sometimes that so little good results from it, we have no criterion in this. If we could see our own light as the Masters to whom we aspire can see it, we should often be surprised at the kind and extent of the good we have done when there is no ostensible proof of it.

Now the assurance which this Master quotation gives us, that our thought and action often produce greater results than we are conscious of, can also be taken as a subtle directive to us. It can take the character of a personal exhortation: *Seek more light!* We should not really *need* this directive. It should be the central aim of our life on the Path, the attainment of more inner light. It could urge us to a persistent effort to bring about a fusion of the light of the mind with the light of the inner spiritual self which is ever present and awaiting recognition. Our mystical studies point the way.

At the same time, I should be inclined to qualify this advice with a kind of warning. It is very natural that search of this kind can be pursued with too much enthusiasm. We must not forget that action on this Path produces reaction, and if the action is tense, so will be the reaction upon the life of the aspirant. It is not for nothing that Masters of the Path have so often counseled aspirants to learn how to wait; to set a time limit for this or that attainment can be very disappointing. There can be no sudden leaps into the region of miracles. There are no soul-destroying examinations set, which must be passed this year or next, or the pupil will be sent down. I do not say that results almost miraculous are not sometimes accomplished—our quotation suggests they are—but it is not at all certain that we shall be conscious of them or of the value of them.

We so often speak and act better than we know. That in itself is of great significance. It means that out of the attained wisdom of the present and past cycles of life, there spontaneously comes forth the latent, light-filled experience which others have drawn forth intuitionally from us. I will give you a concrete instance of this. A member once confided to me a lifelong type of mental aberration he had which often made him fear for his sanity. I felt at the time that all he needed was a clear understanding and appreciation of borderline conditions. I sent him a book for this purpose. Later, when I had forgotten the case, he wrote me that he had waited all his life for that book. Do you wonder that I have so often stressed in writings our paramount need for deeper understanding and compassion in touching other lives?

The real Rosicrucian, worthy of that ancient title, can never be content with platitudes and the superficialities of life. The lives of those he is privileged to contact on the Way must kindle the deep fire of the heart and inspire him to an intimate sharing in a human need. We can hasten this process by persistently looking upward to the spiritual self, the presiding soul, which overshadows and inspires the coordinated personality during periods of meditation and from that vantage point of withdrawal, entering gradually at will into a sphere of soundless contemplation, in which the higher powers can bestow upon us deeper and mystical insight.

It would be a mistake to think of the early Rosicrucians as merely men of action. They were far more than that. They were expert contemplatives. They lived an unseen and unknown life of inner communion. That was the source of their power. From *that* they derived their vision. Their objective life was so completely aligned with the contemplative life that the ordinary accepted standards of speech and action were often entirely ignored, lost sight of, before the illumination and direction of the inward light and inspiration of the soul.

It is little wonder that they were men in direct conflict with their contemporaries in thought and expression and sometimes had to pay dearly for their spiritual ascendancy, but contemplatives they were *first* and men of unique speech and action *afterwards.* That is what is needed today in a disjointed, distracted, and superficially active world. Never before so much as now do we need to retreat within, beyond the frontiers of the sorry babel of contesting tongues and the all-absorbing adventures of would-be masters of outer space to the infinite spaces of the wise silence of the soul, where reside the first and last secrets of our incarnation.

Let us then discard the idea that we meet together merely for the pleasure of social intercourse and seek the deeper level of a united-heart contact, which shall throw light upon the profound issues and meaning of our incarnation and enable us to bring to others a breath of vision and a power of service which are the aim and end of all our culture on the Path.

THE CONFLICT OF OPPOSITES

Lecture delivered 1960

The Greek philosopher Heraclitus regarded the universe as a ceaseless conflict of opposites. "War," he said, "is the father of all." I do not interpret this term "war" as applicable to the insane conflicts between nations, as we too painfully know and remember them. It has for us, and had no doubt for Heraclitus, a far more intimate and continuous applicability to the opposition and struggle of forces within man on his journey through life, for, if life itself from early years to late is not a conflict of opposites, I do not know what else it is. I think that the more you study your own life with insight and impartiality, you will find this conflict of the opposites operating right through it. You will find that it has confronted you with unending problems of adjustment, a constant challenge to the best you believe in, know, and can do. It is the law of life, and there is no escape from it at this point of our evolution. Moreover, if we expect life to bear fruit in good works, nothing less than the conflict of opposites will produce them.

The young aspirant, setting out in the warm enthusiasm of early anticipation on the Path, may not regard this mature a judgment too favorably. He will not be inclined to view his new venture in a search for more knowledge in any other way, than he would devotion to a science, an art, or to commerce as just another interest in a different direction, even as a possible shortcut to a kind of "super manhood."

Now one thing which is undoubtedly responsible for an aspirant assuming this attitude towards his studies is the number of books being published under arresting titles and purporting to teach some marvelous new system of development. He cannot be expected to take the measure of these books at a glance which the experience of a mature student enables him to do.

A great artist said, "Man cannot be taught to compose or to invent, but he can become a good copyist," and most of the books of the present-time cults are but poorly disguised replicas of half a dozen originals, which came direct from the mind of God and which can never be added to by busy little minds who lust after recognition and fame. This is a hint to the young aspirant to sharpen his critical faculties, that he may learn to discern early rather than late that far from all those who cry loudly, "Master, Master," have entered within His auric influence. One need only place, for instance, the modern books on Yoga, Buddhism, and many other systems of thought alongside the original standard expositions and techniques to note from whence the moderns derive the incentive to chart new and short paths to the promised land. The occult press reminds me, to compare small things with large, of the glut of novels on the art of detection, the original masters of which were Poe and Doyle, whom none have improved upon or equaled since they wrote.

But once the aspirant is aware of this modern trend in literature, bearing upon some aspects of his studies, he will do well to become a severe critic of what is presented to him and refuse to be misled by these deceptive lights and look to the masters of his science who have shown the way because they have trodden and understood it. Under the guidance of those proficients, he will soon realize that the Mystic Way is not a flower garden bedecked with roses, which charm the sense and make the journey to the mountaintop a pleasant dream. He will find that life can play havoc with dreams. He will find that life can be and should become the Cross of Christ in action. Until he does realize that, he is but dreaming.

It is not my wish to damp the enthusiasm of the aspirant, but let it be a rational enthusiasm. Reason and aspiration are not

THE WAY OF THE HEART

contradictions. They can exist together, and the closer their association, the sounder and surer will be his development. He will come to appreciate the view of Heraclitus that, "Life on the Path is a ceaseless conflict of opposites." Why should this be so? Because fundamentally, esoteric unfoldment is never an uneventful progress along a straight line. It ever proceeds in spirals. We return again and again, apparently to where we were, but a little wiser on each spiral through perfectly mundane experiences which force the truth of life upon us. It is up to the aspirant to achieve all he can upon each spiral of the way. He will not do this by seizing upon and giving allegiance to every book that promises to give him an unprecedented lift into a revelation of the facts of the universal intention.

It is surprising how many writers profess to lucidly interpret the minds of the Masters for us and put us right. Until we are able to interpret a little for ourselves and drop these masqueraders by the wayside, our advancement lies in facing the circumstances which have placed us just where we are and which hold the secret of our individual progress. It is astonishing how many aspirants place their whole faith in this or that so-called teacher, in this new cult and that, but it is not astonishing to find them after a few months or years just as irrationally enthusiastic in another direction in the expectancy that, at last, they have found what they sought in the beginning. It is the circumstances of life, the living intimately the present hour, which teaches what we are made of, what we can do and striving to do it, which reveals the soul's deeper life.

If I were asked what is the cause of this waywardness and subsequent disillusionment often noted in the life of the aspirant, I would say he has not comprehended the deeper meaning of Heraclitus in his statement that, "War is the father of all." It is a statement he is likely to question, but is it true? When people today are asking for a world at peace, the idea that war presides over all is neither encouraging nor palatable. We have had enough of it exoterically, but esoterically we really need more of it. Indeed, it has been said that we need crises in life if we are to grow, and if the aspirant is not aware of any in his life, he should precipitate them. That is another statement which sounds very discomforting. Nevertheless, it is true. He who never has to face difficulties and trials, challenges to his strength of character, his insight, foresight, and impartiality, may be sure that he is not in training to face the issues and take up the kind of charge a Master would be likely to place upon him. Why, the disciple I want the aspirant to become carries the marks of all this, written indelibly in him. He has not been called a battle-scarred warrior without good reason.

If we can read the signs rightly, we shall always find them stamped by the fire of the soul itself upon him, even if we do not know all they signify. Yet if we not merely look, but deeply think, we shall come to realize what they mean. War on the three planes of endeavor has done its best and its worst to make the mature disciple what he is. We shall find that all along the way he has been faced with one crisis after another, and if he had not surmounted spiral after spiral under the accumulating tension of these crises, with his own wounded hands, he would never stand where he is.

You will pardon my earnestness, but I cannot regard this pursuit of higher culture, to which we have consciously and deliberately called ourselves, in any other way. In a sense, it is something different and apart from the whole of life around us yet at the same time compels us to become more and more a part of it. Is not this multifarious life a profoundly serious thing, an obligation laid upon us to be careful how we meet and use it? Is it not like a firm and warning hand laid upon the heart, demanding from us care, conscientiousness, and right action in dealing with it, when we see what utter chaos thousands make of it? That is why we are apart from it and yet have to work with and for it.

Here we have the conflict of opposites in its most crucial aspect, a two-way momentum of the life of the serious and aspiring soul and of the life of the world which will have none of it, and this continuous effort at right adjustment impresses upon us a further truth, that we bring ourselves, whether we know it or not, face to face with those higher beings who have prompted and guided us to secure their cooperation. For what purpose? Literally, as we shall later realize, to inscribe the life of the cross in our members with unrelenting compassion, to the end that we radiate unconsciously the co-active influence of all the soul has known and suffered through the cycles during its ascent to their presence, an influence which will unerringly reach and change the lives of others with whom we associate, even in the ordinary ways of life.

It will be understood that I do not discountenance the value of books and teachings of the right kind, but the aspirant has to live these out experimentally on all the planes of life and in all his members. When we see a first-class athlete in demonstration, we cannot fail to realize the unique discipline of body and mind the years have demanded of him. It is the same with a master artist. Complete devotion and one-pointed application have brought them through all the crises incidental to a perfection of technique. There has been no short-cut, no neglect of detail, no sharing of difficulty and responsibility, but a ready and complete acceptance of life and circumstance to the one end of the mastery sought.

It may be thought that I am suggesting what few can give. I am viewing our aim and purpose from a high level, for what ultimate satisfaction can there be in flitting through life playing with the toys which amuse the millions until a reckoning of the swift years has to be faced, and the final opportunities of a cycle are seen to be beyond reach? The time is rapidly passing, if it has not already passed, when simply reading about the path is of major importance. Since the dawn of the New Thought movement in Britain at the beginning of the century, libraries of literature on mind power have become the property of millions. How much has it done to create a new world? With all this reading after half a century, we should be hard put to it, to show any very prolific results from it, esoterically speaking.

It is something, but it is not enough, to say that results must be there, hidden from us, in the background of life. That really satisfies nobody nor helps anybody, and to those who do not like this argument, I would say, they will soon see it demonstrated by the real students of this generation now coming to the front; silent, self-styled saints who are found in some of the so-called esoteric societies of today, the self-righteous ones who have God to themselves, well within the confines of their societies, misty-eyed theorists who are expecting the appearance of a Christ in their midst to prove their own theories correct and work miracles for them. These and such as these, the keen and demanding young minds now questioning and seeking Light, will leave at the end of the queue. They will push back for themselves the frontiers to liberation of the soul with their own eager hands, revealing a path which only genius has had the courage to tread hitherto.

Swift once said, "There never appear more than five or six men of genius in an age, but if they were united the world could not stand before them." Well, if half a dozen illuminated spirits burst upon Britain with the resplendent Light of the Cosmic around them, something would happen in the minds of men. Aspirants, and not only they, would realize that it is the individual who counts, not the weak conformist who runs with the crowd. They would realize that the great need today is for self-discovery, a focusing inward, to tap the resources of the soul.

In one of our advanced grades, it is said, "There comes a time when each seeker who travels the Path must travel alone. One must, sooner or later, work alone in development and cannot depend upon teacher, Master, friend, or lodge companion to assist as in the lower grades of study." This means that up to that point the aspirant has been shown a way of experimental approach, and thereafter he must look for initiation into a higher realm of contact with forces and insight through his awakened and dedicated mind, when his own individual way will be revealed to him. That is the time of testing, and he who has been leaning upon others and depending upon their help all the way will not easily meet that test. Our greatest struggles are always lonely ones. There are steps on the Path which we must take alone, and we should not fear them. We have the testimony of others to this fact and the voice of the ancient prophet confirms it, "I have trodden the wine press alone and, of the people, there was none with me."

I began on a note of conflict within man. I conclude on this same note of conflict, because it is inescapable and demonstrable, for every seeker who pledges himself irrevocably as a servant of the cosmic powers. Directly he gets well onto the Path in purpose and aspiration, he is faced with this universal law of opposites and inner war. It has always been operative in his life, but now he becomes acutely conscious of it. It compels him to reflect, to interrogate himself, to decide. It is of no use for him to leave his decisions to others. He must make his own decisions and take the consequences of them. If he has not that temper of mind, he will move along with the crowd and get nowhere. The Path demands that temper of mind, and the true aspirant will sacrifice much for it and not fear the consequences. He will find the circumstances will come full circle under the set and inflexible will.

The early spirals of the way are often the most difficult. Let them do their worst; and still persist. Yet a little while, a little further, and the light of the soul will be released from its cruel bondage of the past. The mind will receive a new impetus, a new force, a recognition from the Master's own presence which will reveal life in its true perspective and dissipate all doubt of the truth of the way and how to walk in it.

HUMAN IDENTIFICATION

Lecture delivered 1961

For many years your Chapter has accorded me the pleasure of recording a message for the annual conclave of assembled members and visitors, and I am pleased today to add one more message to the series. I have regarded these occasions as special events and to be treated with all seriousness and promise.

Many of the older members I have known personally for many years, prior to these talks and long before the last war. I have known them in character and in action through the ups and downs of a most testing period, and nothing has deflected them from their first pledge of loyalty to the Order. They constitute a fine example for those who have recently become members, for many new faces are appearing among us, both English and from overseas. Our aim is to incorporate these fresh forces into a mainstream of a Chapter life. I want these new members to realize that their part in the Work is not merely to attend or visit, but to fully align themselves with the mental, emotional, and spiritual life which they will find established here.

What our advanced members have found through long experience is that by their dedication to Chapter activities and studies, following the imparted instruction, individual hindrances to their collective and effective working have in good time passed and any necessary readjustments have been made and the harmonious cooperation of all secured. This is a valuable point for emphasis because it eliminates any doubt as to the objectives and any impatience in the realization of them. It has also proved that cooperative Chapter discipline is of first importance in individual evolution and what results may be indicated for this cooperative group association. There has been a marked increase in general sensitivity among members that was to be expected because confined activities of this nature stimulate automatically the etheric disposition of the group and make many unusual contacts possible. This inner awakening, this sensitivity, is apt to be overlooked since it is subtle and unobserved, and does not admit of being defined like more objective results.

The healing capacities of a Chapter have increased during the years with much success through special ministrations given through it. And what is of particular interest is the telepathic and prophetic elements of its work have been strongly in evidence. One of the simplest forms of this is the contacting of correspondents directly and intimately, even to an indication of what has been written, and responding to the contents of correspondence before it has reached us. But such indications of psychic unfoldment should not engross us too much. They should interest us chiefly because they extend our ability in the way of service. This fact of service must be stressed because it lies at the heart of the Rosicrucian life.

The Chapter is not simply a meeting place for members to enjoy personal contact between themselves or to congratulate themselves upon their own progress. Our aim is an ever-expanding service to be carried abroad and to life, and made even noticeable there. If this is ignored for any other angle of self-development, how do we as Rosicrucians differ from so many around us who care nothing for the actual teachings of the higher culture, yet are a blessing to their fellows? A peculiar service of insight and helpfulness should be the distinguishing characteristics of a Rosicrucian. He should be a marked man. He should carry an atmosphere of a distinctive type. His inner life should manifest itself and radiate from him wherever he contacts human life. Is this so with us; or do we carry what we are in knowledge and inward satisfaction well locked up within us and give the troubles and problems of others a wide berth?

Think of the appalling suffering of life on every hand. It is encountered at every step. We may turn away from it because the subject is not a cheerful one. But whichever way you turn, it will confront you. It is written large in the Karma of national and international life and cannot be evaded. Yet there is a whole library of success literature abroad today which urges you to ignore and deny it. Now, what we term *advancement on the Path* means, in the very real and important sense, increasing recognition and understanding of what karmic process means in other lives as well as in our own. The only access to this lies in human identification. You must pass sympathetically into other lives through the process of *spiritual identification.* Until you do that, you cannot begin to interpret the manifold indications and purposes of karmic outworking in your own life or in others.

It is an interesting discovery to make that, in the endeavor to pass beyond the orbit of the personal self into the light of the soul, the personalities of others reveal a greater worth and invite you to a deeper participation in their lives. It is not primarily a love of a personality, but of a soul power struggling to express through it. Not for the personality alone is the friend dear; it is what the opening and compassionate eye and heart sense and see within the personality, who comes to one in perfect trust and anxious inquiry. I refer to the growth of general sensitivity among our members, through their active cooperation in the Chapter activities. This indicates that an ever-widening field of subtle impressions is being contacted, which is either beyond intellectual definition or, if admitting of this, is of so interior a nature that the soul sometimes elects to live silently in the recognition of it and carry the burden of it without utterance.

I believe this to be largely due to registration of the ever-present sorrow of human existence. It does not obstruct activity. *Depression* is not a rightful term for it, although superficial minds may think it that. It is the atmosphere of souls in and out of time.

And if you want a gracious example of it, look to the Masters of life themselves, for you will never partake of their life and vision unless there is much of that receptiveness in you. It softens and suffuses the inner life and is quite apart from the mortal man. I will call it *feeling insight.* It derives only from active and earnest interest in souls until eventually the secret Path and all souls are sensed, and the reaction to that access is that one comes to bear the impress and carry to some degree the unseen burden of the soul of the world.

So keen and insistent is that inflow of the world sense that did not a continuous outflow of the love released within the personality take place? Highly resensitized human nature would ill sustain it. Does this seem to be the striking of a high note for ourselves? Our highest teachings have much to say about it and indicate the way to it. I have but to make a personal and necessary application of it to be in full accord with all that lies beyond the confines of personality.

We see the possibility of it, but the actual experience is a step beyond. That step can be bridged through the power of an active and radiating love. That is a basic and divine fact—and nothing can dethrone it or nullify it. It would decide the advancement of a Chapter to larger objectives. Increasing sensitivity within it is admittedly a matter of some difficulty since it renders the personality more reactive to conditions, not only within the group, but in the world. The prevailing world conditions play upon the sensitive group organism as upon a finely tuned instrument. This is not to be regretted, for it affords opportunity to respond to the heights and depths of human life. It is a step toward universality and knowledge and experience.

We turn from the academic, understood and appreciated, to the demonstrative and executive, to the objectivication of the soul in the world. We become more reactive to the movements of life and find our greatest lessons written there in luminous colors. We shall gain much by shifting the emphasis from a consideration of our goodness or reputation in the eyes of man or master. To the uninitiated this may sound dangerous doctrine, but not to those of us in here. It is surprising to note sometimes what so-called men of the world do in native goodness and self-forgetfulness because they have the soul to do it. We should be the example in that! We may regard our interest and devotion to the Path as height and the key to special privileges, but, as a matter of fact, there is neither height nor depth in real discipleship. There is understanding response to all. But what does this understanding response to all really mean? It means a variety of adjustments to different levels of consciousness.

If, for instance, there comes to us a soul—you observe that I say a *soul*, not a *personality*, because as Rosicrucians we need to get the soul of persons and things, not their appearances—there comes to us a soul rich in love, keen, resolute and balanced, expert in knowledge, discriminative and responsive, then the full accord of your soul can find utterance in that life. There is no hint of suggestion or domination. It is discernment in another of possibilities of new and quick expansion that merits your art and technique, and can bear the force of them. It is not so with all— far from it. It is a kind and measurable response in another which elicits the kind and measured response from yourself. And this varies so considerably that it is impossible for one with a lesser ability and quality of response to realize the applicability of it to another further on in evolution.

Experience in the Chapter can teach us so much, even by contrast! Open your morning paper and note the trend of things for a day, and what do you find? The everlasting wrangling of politicians, those clever saviors of the world; the undisciplined tempers and ravings of men of high estate, only high financially; and those of low estate—the mob. From a cultural point of view, both are a reproach and a warning; from the spiritual point of view, they are a menace.

Then you make a periodical retreat into the peace and tranquillity of your Chapter for quiet reflection. You seek to carry that healing atmosphere away with you as a daily panacea. You have a sense of being overshadowed by it because the collective status and tenor of the Chapter life finds reflection in oneself; hence, your personal responsiblity in it. You help to make it what it is, both in character and function, by the prevailing attitude of your inherent nature, your emotional and mental life, and your spiritual aspiration. This is something really worthy of your time and interest, for it makes you not only a live unit in the group capacity, but a beneficent force for good in everyday life.

EXPANSION OF KNOWLEDGE

Lecture delivered 1962

Your Chapter came into existence quietly and unpretentiously, and if its voice and action have increased in volume and extent through the years and attracted international attention, that is only what we hoped and expected of it. Not that it has been smooth sailing; quite the reverse, but the unrelaxing concentration and devotion you have given have wrought many a silent miracle of unselfish service. Today we think with affection of those who were with us during those early years and passed through Greater Service, and of those who are still with us and working with the same high purpose.

It was in the year 1954 that I made my first recording for the Chapter. You may remember that I made particular reference in it to the Code of Life given in the Manual. I also referred specifically to the opening concurrences of the Mandamus monographs consisting of quotations from the works of famous thinkers of the past, only one of whom was a Rosicrucian. But all of them were men of profound thought and meditation, whose names are famous in the world's literature as instructors and enlighteners of their fellowmen. The characters mentioned were Bacon, Kant, Schiller, Woolman, Emerson, and Pascal.

Those of us who were interested to study at least some of the works of these thinkers and writers do not have any doubt about the vast range of knowledge and instruction, of culture and information contained in them. The same values are, of course, to be found in the works of many of profound genius who were undisputed instructors of the past. The extent of their influence has been universal and immeasurable. Indeed, they constitute the basis of studies in the colleges and universities of note in the civilized world. And if what has been affirmed is true, that the great universities of the world possess, as a whole, practically every form of knowledge known to civilization, then the characters I have noted are certainly to be among them.

Therefore, in view of these facts, I wish to put two or three questions for our consideration. Are we in any way disloyal to our chosen mystical studies in seeking also a knowledge of the highest levels of human thought and philosophical culture reached by the world's master minds? Is it to our loss or gain that we fear or hesitate to acquaint ourselves with the great thinkers and writers of past time?

I have put these questions for a definite reason. They relate to a letter I have received from a responsible officer of our Order— a man of distinctive character, professionally well known, and of studious habit—who is engaged in active work and study with members in an official capacity, and to whom during a discussion with a fellow officer, the latter implied that there was something a bit disloyal in resorting for knowledge outside the published library of the Order. You may imagine the surprise of my friend at a statement of this kind, implying disloyalty in a search for knowledge. His comment to me was that he felt this was similar to the attitude of the Roman church. Moreover, what he would wish would be the privilege of knowing the whole hierarchical plan of creation and his place in it. I may assure you that this did not come to me from a member of your Chapter.

Can we afford to ignore what the mind of man has been inspired to give us through the centuries? If we do ignore it, the fact yet remains that we profit from it every hour of our lives. It has penetrated the very fabric of our daily speech and action through a multitude of unseen channels of influence. Think for a moment what this kind of contracted view of knowledge and education can really mean. If we should confine our reading, for instance, to the published writings of the Rosicrucians available to us and think that loyalty to our studies consists in refusing recognition of the magnificent structures of philosophical thought of the world's recognized genius which have inspired and enriched the student mind through the centuries to the present day, how could we speak with authority within the Temple of Life or meet our opponents in the gate on subjects on which they themselves are well informed and upon which we should be able to throw new light by virtue of having gone beyond many of them in our own researches?

Bacon, we know, is the only acknowledged Rosicrucian mentioned in the list given in the Mandamus monographs, and to him we owe very much. We know that he took all knowledge for his province and that Macaulay, in his critical study, said that Bacon moved the intellects that moved the world. The name of Kant, the illustrious German thinker and philosopher, brings to mind a happy memory, that of a personal friend of fifty years ago, a brilliant German scholar, who after several years' training at Oxford came to my native city to take up a Unitarian ministry. I sometimes attended his church and lectures. He was a profoundly read man, a most gifted speaker, and knew the classics by heart. On one of my visits to him he pointed to the works of Kant on his library shelves and said he had read Kant six times and yet did not understand him. I have never forgotten that uniquely modest confession.

Some of our young men today would no doubt swallow Kant whole in six concise lectures and straightway forget what manner of man he was. However, I do not anticipate many students have the courage today to read Kant six times. They would certainly never master him in their spare moments, but more likely require one or two incarnations. Nevertheless, it can be said that they might profit much from some sections of the work of this gigantic mind if they use their minds to some purpose. And when we think of the mind of Emerson, all comprehending and cosmic in character, whose thought on life and men flashes from his pages like rays of a rising sun! And of the penetrating insight and vision of Pascal, described by an American biographer as one of the greatest men that ever lived.

I would tell the member who talks of disloyalty that if disloyalty there be, it lies with those who are ignorant of these gifted sons of God—not with those who study them. There is very much in the world today which invites sharp criticism from thinking people, and it is getting it. The reason that it is getting it is that thought is free and acknowledges no boundaries. There has never been a time, at least not in this country, when any one or any thing that would fetter thought and its free expression has met with more forthright and devastating criticism. That of course is good. However little we may sometimes like it, or even deplore it, but it does make quick work for one thing in demolishing many inhibitions which have hampered us in the past and still cling to us. And anyone who should suggest limitations to our reading and knowledge must be very insensitive and deeply misread the signs of the times.

The reprinting and publication of literature in every department of life since the war, during which so many of our libraries and repositories of books were destroyed, has increased to an amazing extent. What is of special value is the issue in comparatively cheap editions of the classics and philosophies of the world. Hence, students young and old have immediate access to these treasures of the mind. If some of us still have confined views and think that this tidal wave of universal knowledge need not interest us, I cannot agree. Your whole studies are of a cosmic character. They urge you to explore beyond the limits of your professional and personal circumstances, and never to be afraid of adventurous research and progress.

Why should we not face and interrogate the cosmic knowledge of the three worlds of human endeavor in everyday life? I call it *cosmic* because it embraces practically all that can be known in these three worlds of daily experience. The more extensive our knowledge of it, the greater and the more balanced will be our efforts and competence in our chosen higher studies in the way of comprehension and appreciation and judgment. Nor must we overlook the fact that our inner life needs this nourishment for the extension of its own sphere of operation and influence. Those who have ventured forth into the literatures of the nations, and fortified their minds with the creative ideas of genius in its many manifestations, will bring back something of the fullness and richness of them to the service of the soul.

In your mystical studies it is not simply a matter of reading only. It is rather a prolonged inner occupation, a continuous, though partly unconscious assimilation of thought imparted and accepted in Chapter or privately. I know an interest in general literature falls within a different category, but if we wish to make a firm impact upon those of intelligence and intellect around us, and whom we contact in business and professional and private life—and often unexpectedly—nothing will so fortify us in our approach and use of the opportunities of contact as a versatile background of knowledge acquired through wide reading. I am far from thinking that every aspirant will be inclined to have the leisure to pursue this kind of ideal for himself. But I am assuming that some are able and will find time for it, especially among those of more mature years who realize the value of this culture, being assured of the latent possibilities of the mind awaiting disclosure.

An historian has said, "We must constantly revert in order to reorient ourselves." There is truth in that remark. It is a hint to look back as well as forward. For if we believe there are immensities of knowledge lying before us and awaiting discovery, we know there are immensities of knowledge lying *behind* us—and their discovery is within reach.

Perhaps one of the most valuable and interesting avenues for exploration is the history of nations, and especially the biographies of great characters who left their mark upon them. And what is of foremost import to us is not only what these characters did in the shaping of their times and ours, but what they were. It is there we can meet the deep essence of an historical period with the minds that made it. In translating ourselves and psychically living in such a period through our own developed sensitivity, a door may open to us apprising us of karmic links and relationships only awaiting our attention and discovery. Karmic forces are moving quietly and quickly. Their secrets await our recognition; our own evolving and immediate future is related there within this or that historical period; and our own sensitivity and intuitional insight can lead to many individual revelations provided we make an endeavor, in the words of Hermetic literature, *to expand ourselves to the magnitude of all existence.*

I believe these thoughts will appeal to your reason and your intuition, and you will agree with me that our aim should be the expansion of our knowledge, not its limitation. You will remember that while the present values of mysticism and spirituality in the world are at a low ebb, the tide of general and scientific knowledge is running high. It is so powerful and swift that the student mind can scarcely adjust to and assimilate it. Therefore, the mystical student should face that truth and interpret for himself just what that means to him. He will realize that the world of education around him is equipping its untold numbers of eager aspirants to knowledge in every field of information obtainable to research. And if he is wise, he will endeavor to participate to some degree in this worldwide movement of the mind of man and resolve to round out his development for the purpose of effective service.

THE VALUE OF GROUP SERVICE
Lecture delivered 1964

The Pythagoras Chapter is to be congratulated on initiating this, the first combined rally to be held in this country. For some years, as you know, we have been engaged in the endeavor to extend our work by increasing membership and bringing the various Chapters into prominence. Groups are dominant today. Since the last war, which compelled the formation of all kinds of groups on cooperative labors and service, the idea has grown rapidly until now, groups of every description are rampant, many good and some very bad, but they do indicate the strong tendency of the time to associate in groups and work in and extend them.

But when we consider our work in the Chapters, extension is not everything. First of all, why do we associate in them? Because we want something which the orthodox religions and philosophies cannot supply, and science, which has said and done some smart things, is also behind the times as we soon come to realize in our teachings. So in our Chapters, we study together to inform ourselves in matters which are beyond the scope of science and religion. Study should be an essential element also in the private life of a member, but he enters a different atmosphere and incurs an added responsibility when he becomes a unit in a group organism such as a Chapter.

One of the main requirements of group activity is the elimination of individual purpose in the interest of the whole. You may not like the term, but the fact is, that in working together in a cooperative capacity, there is demanded of the individual an act of self-effacement. You cannot be all yourself when you cooperate with other students for a chosen end. There is usually a good deal in the mental and emotional life which has to submerge if you want harmony and progress. There must be a certain quiescence and interior silence in the individual if the group aura is to be rightly formed and function. The history of Chapter life has proved only too often that the reverse has been the case. Individuals have come in to assert themselves, to demonstrate the extreme value of their own personality, and their subsequent elimination has been necessary in the interests of the Chapter, for the group aura is of fundamental significance. It can be disorganized and its influence curtailed at once, through the presence of inharmonious units in it.

The chief hindrance to the successful working of a Chapter in the past has been this: only some of the members give themselves unreservedly to the esoteric aspect of its activities. If increased knowledge of one's self and of the Path is desired, Chapter life must be taken seriously. It is not enough to belong to a Chapter. The question is, what can you contribute to it? Beyond the actual and factual teaching therein, you should be able to bring your own inward contribution of insight and discovery into direct communication with others. You need to be well informed, and every member should make it his business to acquire wide and useful information bearing upon all aspects of his studies in the Order, even with a view to augmenting and extending them.

That is why I say extension in numbers is not everything. The question for you is, what is the pattern of your esoteric influence there? In imparting your own acquired knowledge in your discussions, your own inspirational technique of service, your own power of healing and giving some measure of comfort and assistance to others in the Chapter who may need these far more than you realize and await your approach to them. Indeed, that is almost the main virtue of group cooperation. If it is not a dynamic and dedicated concentration of the faculties of your inmost self within the Chapter, if you simply come and go, and your influence is not felt there in any beneficent way, you miss the aim of the true Rosicrucian ideal, for the hand of service—which means an expression of your whole personality—should be called into use and find its own special field of operation.

To be a good listener is well, but that does not make you a Rosicrucian. You must make way for the spirit of creation and expression along the lines of your gift, but in such a way that it harmonizes with your group associates. Instances in the various occult groups are too well known to be overlooked of individuals in them who, in spite of their good intentions and conscious of the multiplied power to which all in the groups have access, forget that power and extended knowledge are for their use but to corporate ends, not simply for personal prestige.

For service is at the heart of our activities. That is easily said, but wise cooperation, to render it effective, is another matter. That is why I said you cannot be all yourself in a Chapter. The diversity of types in it, the various karmic limitations and possibilities under which these types have to live and express, demand not only your interest but deep insight and understanding if you would be of any use to them beyond merely social contact. They have prejudices and predilections which national characteristics and praise foster and accentuate, and make adjustments to others difficult. Some are pronounced extroverts, others the opposite, and it takes time and patience to observe these qualities and differences, realize their value and bring them to full expression in the Chapter. That is the special responsibility of the officers. From them, a more specific understanding is to be expected of the selected units in the Chapter in order to promote among them and make them aware of the combined influence and helpfulness of their fellow members.

You will observe that I place much responsibility upon the officers and other representatives in a Chapter for direct personal helpfulness and service to the members in it. I do so because I think it has often been considered sufficient if there is concentration upon the actual teaching given, while the important factor of more intimate contact with members has been overlooked or neglected. It has been considered sufficient if there is an intellectual grasp of problems that arise in the teachings but little concern about the troubled soul behind and wrestling with those problems. Intellectual comprehension is a valuable asset, but emotional depth and sympathetic understanding and receptiveness to need are quite another matter for your consideration, and very often more important. It is a revelation to see how much the heart craves for your insight and loving appreciation, far more than your cleverness in statement of problems.

Your chief aim should be to render this kind of personal service to others, for your work in the Chapter, if it has been of real esoteric value, should have cultivated a degree of sensitivity enabling you to sense, sympathetically, the inner lives of your fellowmen. You need the awakened inspirational quality of mind and heart which can sense and reveal what is within and conditioning the lives of members, and that means to bring into effective use the telepathic and psychometric faculties of the soul which should be familiar to you in the later stages of your studies.

It is not the intellect which should be of paramount interest in a Chapter; it is the life of the indwelling and aspiring soul. It is easy to be well informed and clever today. Factual knowledge confronts us everywhere, in books and on the air, but the soul is missing. That is what many of the new members feel, and the inadequacy of the intellect turns them to us. Therefore, I mark a great difference between a purely intellectual technique of approach and application and a compassionate emotional identification in service. You need in your Chapter life the love of those who are waiting to express it, for the understanding love, which emanates from the heart of group life, can mean a real expansion of consciousness. You need to recognize that there is, here and there, a rich content in humanity, unexpressed and waiting to reveal itself, and only the penetrating light of initiate consciousness, thrown upon it, will invite it to disclose itself.

THE CHAPTER'S PURPOSE

Lecture delivered 1965

We now regard our rally as a unique event here and one which has qualities and a robust thoroughness not to be found elsewhere which mark it as an occasion of exceptional importance.

Only a few years ago, we were visualizing and feeling our way to a new type of convention and interchange of contact with members from far and near, which would give it an enthusiasm and coloring well in advance of the past. Last year's rally for instance, with its variety of well-prepared features given by competent officers, produced most excellent results and demonstrated what can be done when preparation is perfected and the will for success and the purpose of highest service are fully expressed. That which most deeply interested me about the rally was the devoted labor of the officers responsible, revealed in all the features of it, and their sincere cooperation in making the event an outstanding one.

There was a particular fact which I realized had to be taken into consideration when making this recording. It was this: our Chapter does not stand where it did at the time of former rallies. It has grown in character, in mental outlook, in confident personal action, in all-round efficiency, and in attractive influence, all of which not only reacts within the Chapter upon all taking part in it, but it has become memorable in the minds of visiting officers from various parts of the country. It has not only gone rapidly ahead of its former capacities; it has now the self-conscious momentum which is shared by the whole of the staff of officers.

Now this is an ideal we had in mind from the beginning. It has now materialized, but this kind of development does not come from merely desiring it. It comes from purposeful cooperation, understanding, and a determination that the ideal shall be realized. The stature of the officers has grown with their task, and this alone has made their efforts a marked success. There are more capable minds taking responsible office than ever before with new ideas and larger views relating to the purposes of the Chapter as a whole. They have felt the enthusiasm and the ability for concrete action of the senior officers and given wholeheartedly their cooperation to them.

In preparing the many different features of our rally, we have kept in mind a twofold balanced aim—the serious and strictly Rosicrucian aspects of our teaching, as given in the Chapter throughout the year; and also the social and entertaining character of such an occasion. In this way, we seek to focus for the visitors the main purpose of the Chapter for their stimulation and encouragement and to stress the importance of the social aspect which will invite a closer personal contact between them and ensure their cooperation in all the Chapter's activities.

A further factor which we in the Chapter are fully alive to is this: the increasing influence of television in disseminating knowledge of the most varied kinds, the information afforded by experts relating to most aspects of life and conduct, and the consequent enlightenment gained from all this. Much there is to be deplored and decried issuing from the same source, but we know that our members share with the many the enlightenment referred to, and the point I am making is, that in the general increase of knowledge and information all share alike, and this is bound to modify personal views held on the trend and conduct of present daily life. It visibly affects the view of the young members who imbibe the scientific and cultural and other information relayed for them with a positiveness and note of finality which admits of no interrogation or criticism.

To most of this, our teachings can provide a decided corrective, and wherever the views are expressed by members as a kind of challenge to what the monographs teach, it will be our business to meet this challenge and to expound and expand those views by a sound psychological and mystical approach. This kind of challenge is to be expected, and I think will increase among new members today because of the passive acceptance of so much that is relayed to them with that complete assurance and finality I have mentioned. But we know that even the preliminary teachings of our early grades completely undermine many views and statements which are given with the emphasis of authority by those who have no sympathy with the interior and psychic approach to the understanding of self and life which we offer and which would revolutionize the thinking of the misinformed or partially informed members.

What do we envisage for the young members attending this or other Chapters: a life of definite usefulness under the Rosicrucian guidance. We can regard them as a group of eager recruits, willing to qualify under a self-imposed discipline for positions of authority as real servants, for we may be assured that the hierarchy of Masters is not standing still. Its entire personnel is alert and vitally active, well aware of and directly interested in all aspirants who are seeking and following the Path in any of its many stages. They are all within the vision of the hierarchy and will receive help and guidance if they demand it and resolve through meditation and service to attune their lives to the rhythm and aims of the hierarchy.

It is an illusion if they think that their faithful and humble efforts, at whatever stage they may be, can count for little because the higher reaches of the Path appear far beyond them. The humblest aspirant, because of his life and service, may be of exceptional promise in the eyes of the hierarchy, and a few years of special effort will bring him an enlarged consciousness and an inner assurance of recognition. Like nature, the revelations of the Path are many and unpredictable. They come not when actually seeking them but when the mind and heart are made ready for them. This is my word of encouragement for the young aspirant. The world outside will give him no such encouragement. It will leave him to his own dreams and aspirations, and it is up to him to take speedy means to materialize them under the watchful care of those ready to help him.

And what of ourselves, the older members and officers who serve in their various capacities in the work of the Chapter? I think of them with admiration and deep appreciation because of the labors and responsibilities they accept so willingly and so ably discharge, but what urges and sustains them in this task? Fundamentally and deep within, they sense and know the ever-present sorrow and suffering of humanity. That is the keynote of all their labors.

Among humanity there is a prevailing mental chaos, a reaching out for it knows not what, a stumbling, a bewilderment from the onslaught of opinions towards an unknown goal of mental achievement. We are aware of this, because we have to live with it. So much the harder is the task. It calls for courage, perseverance, and untiring application, and the influence of our hierarchical contact alone sustains and guides us. In a word, we have to make our way within a kind of circumscribed circle of upward aspiration. We cannot get much help from outside it. We have to look upward and think upward and draw more and more upon the inspiration of the hierarchy and its readiness to respond to us. Nor must we forget that we believe in the cooperation of those who have gone before us. They left their work here unfinished and only to see more clearly beyond the veil and to cooperate more understandingly and helpfully in the greater things they wish to do and to which we are dedicated.

It will be a sorry thought to think that when the Book of Knowledge was closed for them here, it would not be open for them to continue their advancement with the greater souls in the Cosmic to whom they belong. They have made contacts which we, within our present limitations, are unable to make or only at times, quite unknowingly.

We know that at certain stages of the Path we have to travel alone, but that aloneness is an incident of our sojourn here. There is no aloneness on the other side. We work in closer association than is possible here, and as we each seek here to lift some of the burden of life from human hearts, so shall we do it there, collectively and more effectively. It is a chastening and inspiring thought that the doubts and illusions which hinder and perplex us here will fall away beyond the veil and we shall know, with our departed brothers, what the hierarchical beings have done for us though all of the vicissitudes of life. We must hold on to that thought and most when life seems to close down upon us in its many changing moods and challenges our very faith in unseen help and direction.

Unseen influences are ever with us, whether waking or sleeping; in moments of abstraction, we are well aware of them, but to interpret the nature and significance of them calls for a degree of intuitional sensitivity which has to be cultured for. Yet we have gone a good way towards this objective in our studies and especially in our practice. We have reached a stage when our combined concentrated thought affects very strongly those we seek to help in difficulty or illness. Here we touch the very heart of the Rosicrucian life.

The burden of sorrow often descends upon us through this very act of alleviating the distress of other souls. You remember the scripture which refers to the disciples' lifting a little of the heavy Karma of the world. That lifting means that we are actually taking upon ourselves something of the burden of souls who await deliverance each in his own way and, by reason of our development and willingness to see and accept this, we are made the instruments of blessing and redemption through our deliberate effort but often enough quite unknown to us.

You will not consider these reflections as of a too introspective character. They are of the very nature of our studies and arise naturally from the habit we have cultivated of feeling and seeing below the surface of life and of applying our findings to the problems which beset ourselves and others. We do not believe with some that we have done well, and all that is needed, if we merely read or listen to teachings of the Path. They have to be transfused into the blood of the heart and issue forth as the realized truth of life. Our studies teach us to interrogate life in all its aspects, then we reverse the process and look inward in silent contemplation and receive the deeper truths which only await recognition.

We shall come to realize more and more the effect of the spiral process of development which operates in our lives. This takes place very much unknown to us as we pass on through the years. The foundation having been truly laid, the interrogation of life under the guidance of our studies and the inward contemplation to receive the unfolding truth of them, coupled with the silent passage of time, reveal the changes wrought by our spiral development most clearly in the consciousness that we have outgrown the former, more limited selfhood, have a new scale of values and an assured and confident approach towards all that life decrees for us. The decrees of life bring surprise and change, so different from what we expected, so often opposed to so much we hoped for and felt sure of, yet it is much if we are able to meet all eventualities with insight and composure, for that is perhaps the surest sign of real inner advancement.

Our life in the Chapter has brought us a long way from the early years of self-development of the aspirant to the expanded outlook of mature consciousness, where the true spirit of self-sacrifice asserts its right over us. We must not regret or refuse this, no matter what it demands from us or what it elects to do with us. We may not be known to men in the busy life of the world, but if the sacrificial spirit reigns in our heart, every step of the way is foreseen and known on the inner side and nothing can really prevail against it.

JAKOB BOEHME

Lecture delivered 1966

I have been asked to record a message for your Conclave, and the theme I have in mind is suggested by a magisterial admonition of the well-known mystic Boehme. It is this:

> *Where the road is steepest, thither bend thy steps.*
> *What the world refuses, that take thou upon thyself.*
> *What the world will not do, that do thou. Walk*
> *contrary to the world in all things, thus by the*
> *shortest road shalt thou attain to God.*

There you have, in four pregnant sentences, a reverse of the way of the world in a very large majority of its people. Yet, because we are of a mystical persuasion, with much study and meditation to our credit, we cannot with any sense of superiority shut ourselves off from it, nor have we any right to do so. The very fact that we are a part of it, have to rely upon it, could not exist without it, assures us that, under karmic decrees, we have a duty toward it and must cultivate a love for it, even as we aspire away from it. We have chosen the steepest road for our steps, and it must be steep not simply because of its inherent difficulties, but because there are so few comparatively who are prepared to make any attempt to ascend above the material and intellectual planes of existence to encourage and strengthen our hands.

I do not believe there are more lonely souls in the wide world than those who bend their steps to take the steepest road, day by day, very often as if they were living in a world of strange peoples. Times without number I have met with this in our members. In the midst of the rush of events of everyday life, they have to seize their place and play their part with voices innumerable assailing their ears. Yet within they are solitary units, for as for any communion of thought or word of higher understanding, they might as well be among the people of an unknown tongue or in a desert solitude, but that is a fact of the steepest road, and I doubt if there is a mystic of any standing who could not testify to it.

Well, if it is a fact and a decree of Karma, we have to accept it and thither bend our steps. There is no other way for us, and the only thing which can fortify us during this almost unique quest of ours is that not only others greater than ourselves have gone that way but that we are known within the veil which dims for the moment the clearest vision of them and that we have the sure inner guidance of master minds who know all the technicalities of the Way and the efforts and frustrations encountered in our environment in our resolve to reach them.

"What the world refuses, take thou upon thyself," says Boehme. Every step he mentions is a hard one, and this one means that we deliberately take upon ourselves burdens in life which so many evade, reject, or selfishly ignore because they threaten the ease and leisure of their own sense-bound existence. You know the craving for ease in modern life; you meet it everywhere. The indifference and evasion of responsibility in those who could do and be so much is a staggering rebuff to the first principles of humane living, not to mention the keen demand of spiritual aspiration. That disease of the mind must never infect us.

Yet, I was told of a member who declined to visit another who was dying in hospital because the atmosphere of the place would be bad for him. One would think such a person had never heard of the life of Christ or what Rosicrucianism stands for. If we are afraid of soiling our hands in lifting the burden of distress or need, the hour will surely come when we shall need willing hands to have compassion upon us. I can scarcely understand the mentality of those who think otherwise, especially if they have known anything of the tragedies of war and witnessed the havoc of them. But the world itself is the grand illusion, and its hypnotic influence compels allegiance and refusals of the highest and noblest of that which the soul demands of us are a common and glaring factor of modern life. But when the seership of the Master Seer sees through it all from afar off, and our seership should see it too, can we expect our path to be an easy one? We often expect it to be and think we have merited it because the concealed Karma of our lives seems to act against us, but for our future good, only we cannot see the deeper reasons for it. The admonition is stern enough; it does not spare us; it gives a death blow to negative and weak thinking. Indeed, we should need the awakened heart, the tempered will, and a purposeful soul, to do that which the world refuses.

The next step has the same quality of relentlessness in it, *"What the world would not do, that do thou."* It seems to me that Boehme wrote for our time as well as for his own. He must have seen the need for it then, or he would not have written it. The man of vision does not write merely for his own day. His vision sweeps far along the path of evolution. His inspiration carries him into the very heart of life and into the hearts of men. He understands the cycles of evolution and knows that what has been will be, until mankind rises by its own efforts to higher levels of thought and action. Therefore, he does not hesitate to impose upon us this kind of peremptory mandate although it counters abruptly the attitude of the world and lays the responsibility and circumstances arising from it upon us. It is clear that Boehme wrote for the strong soul, not for the weak and vacillating one. One would think that when he wrote this, he did so after a lifelong contemplation and following of the life of Christ. There is the same austerity, the same certitude, the same ascension of all the powers of the soul to the plane of divinity.

Am I going too far in describing the world as "The Grand Illusion?" Boehme leaves us in no doubt as to what he thought it was. His admonition is but a brief direction to the student to make a daily application of it and unveil the illusion for himself. Have not other great authorities affirmed the same? In a famous spiritual classic of the East, written centuries ago, we have this:

> *Know that this revolving world is a wheel of delu-*
> *sion, and the human heart is like its nave or axis. By*
> *its continuous rotation, it produces all this deluson*
> *within its circumference. If, by your manly extertions,*
> *you would put a stop to this motion in the center of*
> *your feeling and desires, you will cause the revolu-*
> *tions of the great circle of delusion to cease.*

That turns the accepted materialistic attitude to the world upside down. It reverses completely the value of the eternal masquerade around us. The sorry thing about it is that we ourselves help to make "The Grand Illusion." We endow it with being and substance in our own minds, but as the advanced psychology of today ventures to affirm, "the world" means how we view the world, our attitude to the world, and can be regarded as our world, our presentation of it. But, in itself the world is indifferent, and it is entirely our acceptance or denial which gives it the character of reality or unreality.

Psychology, therefore, is feeling its way along the frontiers of the province of mysticism. Its most formidable problem now confronts it, since it has to reckon with the spiritual revelations of the ancient East and the mystical assertions of the awakening West. Between the East and the West there is no conflict, but Boehme, and many others before and after him, are still the pioneers of thought in the vanguard of spiritual evolution, and science is beginning to recognize this.

Boehme's conclusion, *"Walk contrary to the world in all things, thus by the shortest road shalt thou attain to God,"* is the crowning assertion of all and touches the highest pinnacle of the mystical path. I invite you to reflect upon it, and try to visualize just what it means. It would appear to demand the outright renunciation of the world, but Boehme was too far-seeing and wise to advocate a rigid compliance with the written word instead of entering into the spirit of it. He knew very well that we are too much a living part of the world and dependent upon it and that a link of destiny has set us in it, that the opposing forces of it become a constant stimulus to rise above them and, in so doing, exert a beneficent influence in other lives. His admonition urges us to reverse our accustomed attitudes and assessments of persons and circumstances and regard the world from a new angle of vision. He exhorts us to realize that this phantasmagoria around us weaves a veil of illusion so cleverly that we shall never know it for that it is until thought and action and emotion are brought under the searchlight of spiritual perception.

It has been said that if we met an adept in the flesh, we should be unable to recognize him. That may be so, but we should be very dense if we did not think and feel differently after meeting him, and our meeting with Boehme should not leave us quite the same as before we met him. We may not immediately recognize "The Grand Illusion" in many of the forms it presents to us, but our cultivated spiritual senses should be *swift* to penetrate and unmask them.

A man can only write what he is on this Path, and the fact that Boehme wrote this admonition is testimony to me that he had experienced what he wrote. We have not attained it, and I doubt if we shall, as long as we live in the world as it is, but it is the true mystical Path as the Masters know and live it, and our efforts to follow it, however much we fall short of it, is all that is expected of us and will bring us nearer to them.

COMPASSION IN THE HEART

Lecture delivered 1967

You have very kindly given my name to your Chapter, and I take this opportunity of thanking you for your appreciation of my work in the Order. My mission in that work has been not to lay down rules and principles, but to inspire and encourage in pursuing what the training of the Path requires of us.

Briefly defined, a Conclave is a meeting of a group with shared or specialized interests. Therefore, we might ask ourselves, what are these specialized interests we should be sharing? I personally have no doubt what they should be, and I ask, "Do they produce not merely a wish to meet together like an ordinary club or a literary society but a deep personal desire and intention to do something worthwhile in the world? For that is what a Conclave of this nature should do, but if, on its conclusion, we leave it in the same frame of mind as that in which we entered it, has it really been an adventure in spirit or merely a social contact? Social contacts are all very well, and they can be had everyday without seeking for them, but we should be after something far more serious and profitable.

Everyone in this Conclave should be fully aware that we shall obtain little on the path of higher culture without a live persistency and strenuous research, because the hidden life of the soul will only reveal itself before a concentrated and dedicated purpose, and in a Conclave we should be intent on one thing and be of one purpose. The social aspect should be of secondary importance. I am persuaded that it is often made of first importance to many. I am not decrying social activities, but they should have a very subordinate place in the minds of the members.

I have been prompted to these comments since it was recently put to me by a responsible officer that much of our effort in group life is directed to social events and occasions rather than to one-pointed Rosicrucian activities. There seems to be justification for this view judging by the mounting interest in these occasions and the noticeable enthusiastic anticipation shown when they are publicized. We shall little impress the present or the future in this way!

We may well recall the lives of the early Rosicrucians if we want an example of how they approached the life of the Path. The earnestness, seriousness, and dignity which characterized all they did and wrote is a flaming challenge to our time, and in the sessions of a Conclave we should endeavor to infuse at least something of the same spirit. There should be mutual interrogation, deep understanding of the nature and purpose of the studies officially promulgated, and a revealing among yourselves of various aspects of your inner selves. A door should be thrown open to the inner self and an endeavor made for a deeper communion of soul with soul.

This nation of ours was, not so very long ago, one of the most insular of nations. It took two shattering wars to crack the shell of our insularity, and that only happened under the hard blows of fate after the feet of the nation had been washed in the blood of its heart. That memory should be enough to make us consider whether, even at this late day, we can fathom the depth of that remarkable rule in the scripture, "Before the soul can stand in the presence of the Master, its feet must be washed in the blood of the heart." It is a rule that a fresh aspirant might quickly pass over and try to forget. He will think its tone ominous and forbidding. Yet, this is a rule inscribed in his own heart which will bar his way to the highest communion until it becomes a fact in his own experience. What is more, it will bar the way of those beyond the status of aspirant until they come to know themselves very thoroughly and understand what life has done and is doing to them psychologically, and why.

Yet, that shedding of the nation's blood did us a great service in this respect: disappointment, suffering, and fear drew its people closer together. Barriers of long standing fell away, and there ensued a great sharing of interests on every hand, from the lowest to the highest, and the deeply rooted insularity which strongly marked this nation was wiped out. We need only look around us today to note how far and in what ways this drastic change has penetrated. It has come, symbolically, through the compulsory and, later, the spontaneous outpouring of the blood of the heart. You may doubt or fail to see the application of this, but the change from insularity to a sharing of interests, on a vast scale, meant a destined release in diverse degrees from an individual bondage.

We know what that release has done for a large percentage of people. It has freed them from much but not elevated them. It has lowered their standard and their value. They are no example to the earnest aspirant. That fact in itself is almost enough to make us retain our insularity and shun the rest. Where there is neither sympathy nor understanding, scarcely even toleration, that is no invitation to us to declare our ideal and purpose. But we, looking to the inner life, should not have needed that release. Many of us did not; we knew what was coming before the first phase of the war struck us. We had already shed much of our insularity through the studies of years of research. We have to rest and progress further on that. I have said it before, and I say it now with renewed emphasis: We shall receive no encouragement from outside, neither from government, church, or society. So much the more imperative is it that we find encouragement within ourselves.

The tide of interest in the mystical life has been against us, in the main, all through this century, and there is not one arresting sign that the tide is turning. Of worldly success in all its manifold forms there is much to acknowledge. Secular knowledge abounds and increases daily to enchain the mind of men more firmly to the temporal. Our so-called education is defeating itself in urging and compelling students to an assimilation and mastery of knowledge for which they have no love but only a perfunctory interest and for which they lack the capability to apply to any useful purpose. The release from one kind of bondage has forced the mind of man to take a hasty refuge in another. His own cleverness has imprisoned him, within a life of form, and he refuses to believe in any possibility of development outside of it.

Our studies lead us in a different direction. If we have shed our insularity in favor of a sharing of interests, that should not mean a mild surrender of our individuality and becoming imitators of one another. Nothing creative or original can come of merely following, yet that often happens in group work. Whereas, we want creative thinking, creative ideas, a bringing out of a soul life within us instead of allowing it to sleep through an incarnation. We should rededicate ourselves again and again with a resolve to pursue the harder way to our self-discovery. Our sharing of interests should drive us inwards, not outwards. Even the social aspects we engage in should minister to that end. We might engage in a reasonable and healthy introspection and remembering that we are what Karma has made us, make a sober assessment, not an inflated one, of what this equipment and the circumstances in which we are, will permit us to do. We should be willing to be different, somewhat out of step with the time, and bring our strength to trial, for the inner self has possibilities, the depths of which we have not yet sounded.

Within this self, we stand as a central point between the unceasing movement of two waves of evolution. One is behind us and comprises the consummation of all our past cycles of incarnation. That stretch of hidden past history conditions us. We have made it and cannot alter it, although it can be modified to some extent and rearranged by a master hand for a specialized purpose if the kind of karmic content to be adjusted admits of it. Therefore, whatever our Karma has brought us in body and mind, in soul and circumstance, we do well to accept it and determine to build upon it. Whether long or short, we have to fulfill its term with a tempered will which can carry us through, not austerely, but remembering the privilege accorded us; to become a servant of the cosmic powers, worthy of the name. If there is relentlessness in the will, there should be compassion in the heart. Both are needed and demanded for a balanced development, and that is always the aim of a disciple of any note. The other wave approaches us from the future, with all its opportunities of exceptional advancement in expanding consciousness, if we are awake to them. We stand at a center, conscious of what life has made us, regretting nothing, because only on that foundation shall we gain the insight and strength of will to face higher initiations of consciousness.

Here, for example, is a member questioning and lamenting, as he well might, the purpose of the Dark Night of the Soul which has come down upon him, but he should be glad that the burden of the incarnations has made him worthy of the trial. Thrown back upon himself, he can see himself as he is and come to realize that the darkness is but the shadow of the Light which awaits him. So it is with every other testing experience which emerges from the silent past demanding recognition and fulfillment. We shall only be ready to meet them and profit from them, understand them, overcome them, or ascend above them if we have drilled ourselves unremittingly to that end.

I refer to communion of soul with soul because only so can members hope to really know one another. We shall never know others if we concentrate mainly upon the acting personification of them in everyday life. The peculiar action of Karma requires this of us. What impresses one is the unexpectedness of the outworking of Karma in lives, pressing forward to its destined fulfillment in so many strange and mysterious ways. We need the inwardness, the sensitiveness, in our contacts to enable us to sense the meaning and drift of phases of experience taking place in them. The mystical life should equip us to penetrate behind the scenes immediately obvious to common observation.

A member recently touched this point very deeply to me, remarking that when he contacted another to assist him, he was quite unable to recall afterwards the many details which a superficial analysis of character would reveal. He was almost entirely occupied with the soul life of the other reflecting itself within him. Those of us who have been pursuing these studies for a long time might endeavor after this kind of perspective, for there is all the difference in the world between contacting and conversing with a person and, under the cultivated impressionableness of his own maturity of soul, entering into a spiritual communion with him.

Obviously, for this, we must have spiritual height and perspective. This may seem to be asking much, but if we are mindful of our studies of years, we should not wish to be noted merely for standing firm but for passing onward to higher ground. We must never forget what the earlier Rosicrucians were, to whom we sometimes refer. They were seers of no mean order. They had extraordinary, intuitive, and spiritual insight. It was precisely because they cultivated and exercised these gifts that they attracted to themselves the obloquy and opposition of governments and authorities who would not tolerate these gifts of the gods among them. And, I know of nothing that would so quickly awaken the like opposition and obloquy, or something worse today, than the advent of a similar company of seers with prophecy on their lips and the luminosity of the spirit in their hearts, but I think that is a far-off event.

A LETTER FROM A MEMBER

Lecture delivered 1967

I want to quote to you from a letter received from a member of our Order. She has been a member for very many years, knows our work in this and other countries through her travels abroad, and therefore is competent to express an opinion about our membership and the work of the Order. She says this: "Why does Rosicrucianism make so many people become materialistic (because it does!)? 'It is your life,' somebody said, and what they mean is 'Do what you want and you would like to do.' But is it my life? What are our lives given to us for, really? Not to gratify every wish or desire, of that I am sure. These thoughts have haunted me for some time, and earnest prayer and meditation on the subject of what to do with all I have tried to make of myself brought me to your book."

Now, a letter of that description, written from personal knowledge and inner conviction, demands a definite and searching reply, and I am going to make it. There are many letters we can file and forget but not when they are written in this stringent tone, and if what this member says is so, does it occur to you that we ourselves may help to foster the attitude expressed in this letter? You know there are potencies in the individual aura of each of us, and those potencies on the Path strongly declare themselves. Our thought life cannot be hidden. It travels far and wide. It has telepathic and psychometric qualities. It is known of men, influencing them unconsciously. It is seen and diagnosed by many. And I say to you, if we permit our studies to divert us from the soul life within, thus giving it an objective and secondary interest in our lives, we have much serious thinking to do.

I was interested to note that your present Chapter Master, at her installation, wished to lay more emphasis upon the mystical and esoteric aspects of your work, to which there was a swift response of appreciation from members since, they said, there had been too much of science of late years. Well, is that a bad sign or a good one?

Science has done well of late. It has had the field to itself, but its reign of miracle and terror is slowing down. For years, it has been billowing in upon the shores of time and space, carrying all before it, until it boasted it could run the universe, but now hesitation and doubt are troubling it. It is encountering an unseen obstacle it can neither see, nor understand, nor dispose of. It is confronting, without knowing it, the impregnable confines of the spiritual realm. It is pausing, questioning, considering what more it can do with its clever hands instead of believing it could do all things. In its chagrin, it may still splutter up to the skies and even come back, but the answer is not there. It will not find God or the Hierarchies on the rocky fastnesses of the moon. It may be objected, "But science is not seeking God so will not be disappointed." Precisely so. It is seeking power and domination and the glorification of men and would transform the creation of God into the image of man. Meanwhile, the spirit within man awaits the hour of science's exhaustion and a change of direction.

The domination by science of the modern mind has been so complete that few have had the heart to declare against its boastful, materialistic assurance or the courage to denounce explicitly its impious tendencies and influence. The compelling power of science has had a hypnotic effect upon young minds, and the governments of the day have encouraged and increased it through their alluring talks, books, and advertisements. The older and experienced members are not fogged or sidetracked by these hidden persuasives. They can strip off the insidious glamor. The young and inexperienced minds readily succumb to it.

It has been said that, for me, discipleship is a serious matter. I was interested in that statement and asked myself, "How could discipleship be other than a serious subject?" What subject is worthy of being taken more seriously than that, the whole aim of which is to fit us for contact and cooperation with those Masters of life who have taken the stages of higher evolution, possessed the clear and long-range vision of spiritual consciousness, and who are ever seeking those who show a promise of discipleship in soul development? I know nothing which a student, who wishes to evolve into what merits to be considered an enlightened and spiritual man, should take more seriously. It should be the central aim of all our studies on the path. No matter at what stage we are working or what aspect of studies is engaging us, we should have this purpose firmly in mind, of so preparing ourselves inwardly to be able to receive impressions and guidance from the hierarchical level of spiritual consciousness.

I need not remind you that my correspondent made no specific reference to your Chapter. She had contacted many Chapters and students in her travels, and to quote her further, "Chapters disappointed me terribly and nearly drove me out of the Order." It seems, therefore, that the basic cause of her criticism is of a prevailing tendency to materialism among the members she has contacted. If we inquire, "What is a Rosicrucian," there are ample authorities to enlighten us, but I turn to a brief definition in a modern dictionary, and what does it say—"a member of an organization devoted to esoteric wisdom." If materialistic science is esoteric wisdom, I have yet to meet with it.

But, I have not quite finished with my good correspondent. She had previously written to me as the result of her reading, and I will quote a few lines from her letter. "Lately I am haunted by an urge to rededicate my whole self, body, soul and mind, everything, in a much greater degree than ever before to service." I think you will realize why I have no apology to make for taking discipleship seriously. Here is a member of age, culture, and experience, with a record of long years of mystical devotedness to the work and having had many psychic experiences, thoroughly dedicated to the inner life, a Rosicrucian in spirit and in truth, revealing her own seriousness in the matter of spiritual development on the one hand and on the other declaring the materialistic outlook, the utter lack of dedication in so many of our members she had known, who have nothing in common with her, in mind and aspiration, and with whom harmonious cooperation is impossible. Well, there is a picture, and a true one, taken from life—not from imagination.

Now, I would like to quote to you from a dialogue between the disciple and the Master in Boehme. The Master is teaching the disciple how he may hear the unspeakable words of God and in reply to the disciple's question how he may hear, the Master says this:

> *When both thy intellect and will are quiet and passive to the impressions of the internal word and spirit, and when thy soul is winged up and above that which is temporal, the outward senses and the imagination being locked up by Holy abstraction, then the eternal hearing, seeing, and speaking will be revealed in thee.*

That touches us today at its highest and best. That is discipleship and given in our grades of teaching, for disciples we are, or should be, with full emphasis upon the esoteric aspect in mind and effort. It is not an easy Path, and that is why so many shun it, even when they think they are on it, but lip service is of no value here. A price must be paid for it, and it will mean much. For one thing, life will not turn smoothly, happily, and carelessly. It will bring the whole man to attention, and how! There will be times of trial, times of change and readjustment. The man that was can no longer meet the occasion. He will demand deeper truth and enter into it, and only when he can say, with my correspondent, "I am haunted by an urge to rededicate my whole self, body, soul and mind, everything, in a much greater degree than ever before to service," will you know what discipleship really is.

I have, on many occasions, spoken and written strongly about the general drift in modern life, but let me say, I have never been ignorant of, or slow to recognize, the good influences in our midst; the work of those who have consistently done and are doing their best to be a light and leading to the younger generation. And unfortunate as it is that Chapter life, wherever it may be, and the name of Rosicrucianism should be a legitimate target for pointed criticism and to the effect that its tendency is to make its adherents materialistic, lays a responsibility upon your Chapter *and others* to ascertain the ground of this criticism. In your own Chapter, as before said, it is asserted by members that science has been too much in evidence. If that is so, the influence is that a materialistic tendency has crept in, which is objectionable and the reverse of esoteric, and a further influence must be made that the inner life, the life of the spirit, is not given its demanding expression. It is for us to direct attention dynamically and interests fundamentally to the inner life as in the higher-grade teaching, not to the making of scientists. That is not the objective of Chapter or the Order, and if it is made so, then we shall certainly neither attract mystical or spiritual men or women—we shall repel them.

As members of a Chapter which has a most creditable history and is well known here and abroad, we might ask ourselves, "Where are we placing the emphasis in life in our studies?" Is it upon the accumulation of facts, scientific or otherwise, the main object of which is to convert a student into a kind of third-class encyclopedia for the ignorant to admire and emulate, or to have a nimble cleverness of tongue to give a stereotyped answer about all things to all men, or to make our borrowed learning a passport to a sounding impression upon our fellowmen? Is it these and similar temporalities which we aim at, or is there a place for the action of the spirit within us to fix our eyes elsewhere, and put the emphasis upon spiritual vision and realities, enabling us to view life and our associates from a higher level of consciousness, to see their anxious need and minister to it, for this is the true Rosicrucian mission?

Therefore, the final thought I would leave with you is this: We cannot do what we like with our lives in the name of materialism or science without incurring the penalties of an ever-present destiny. The spirit of man waits in the wise silence for our recognition and our cooperation and, at the appointed time, will compel them.

THOMAS À KEMPIS

Lecture delivered 1968

It is well known that *The Imitation of Christ* has been translated into more languages than any other book with the exception of the Bible. Within ten years of the author's death, there have been published eighty editions of it. In 1399 Thomas à Kempis, the writer of it, was admitted into a Augustinian convent and there he lived a secluded life writing sermons, hymns, and pious tracts, treating of the monastic and Christian life, in addition to several biographies. The most celebrated of his works is *The Imitation*, obviously the work of a contemplative, for it breathes of the quietness and peace of the cloister.

With its combination of simple faith and mysticism, it has never ceased to appeal to all manner of men and women of every conceivable religious and mystical persuasion. When a devotional book makes an universal appeal to the human heart, as this book has done for several centuries, we may be sure that it is the offspring of divine inspiration and has a profound message and meaning for us.

It is related of Pascal, that when about to write, he used to kneel down and pray to the Infinite Being so to subdue every part of him unto itself, that when he was thus brought low, the Divine Force might enter into him. By self-abasement, he prepared himself for the receiving of inspirations. That is the attitude we must have if we wish to profit from *The Imitation*, then a door softly opens into Temple of Holiness. The music of the voice of the disciple kneeling before the altar falls upon our ears. We forget what we are and listen to a voice of yearning compassion telling us what we might become, and when we pass out into the strident world, we carry the tones of that voice within us and we know that it is attuned with the Spirit of Christ.

In these days we hear very much about the revelations of psychoanalysis, psychology, and psychiatry and other allied methods of scientific probings of the sacred precincts of personality and soul, yet, when all is said and done, where do we stand? We stand face to face with our own secret thinking and consequent outward action. If our thinking conforms to the Law of Christ within us, there is a plain and lighted way to our action in the world, and the fears, inhibitions, and complexes which haunt the majority and provide a rich source of enterprise for clinics and professors pass away like mist before the rising sun.

We do not think of the author of *The Imitation* as a psychologist, a psychoanalyst, or a psychiatrist, nor has he ever been described as either, but he is greater than any of them. He has looked into the heart, mind, and soul of man from the vantage point of a seer illumined by the Consciousness of Christ, uncovered every palpable or lurking weakness of mortal man, and revealed the way to immortal selfhood.

The rare quality of à Kempis is that he reveals the unexampled genius of a man possessed with a passion for Christ. From the first words to the last of his book, we are impressed with the unrestrained influence of a man who is overwhelmingly possessed with the presence of Christ, who has seen, lived, and communed with Christ. The whole book revolves around the one central theme which absorbs him: of man, helpless, broken, buffeted, and perplexed by his own unreclaimed nature, which has turned away from or forgotten the divine presence within him; of man unredeemed and blinded through absorption in the passing phantasmagoria of the life of the world; and of the challenging and sadly compassionate figure of Christ ever before his vision and pointing the way which He had trodden in defiance of all the difficulties, hindrances, and treacheries which the Karma of the world could set against Him.

I question whether there is any teaching in any other book of devotion which so truly epitomizes the path of discipleship as we know it, as it is presented in the chapter entitled, "Of the King's Highway of the Holy Cross," in the second book on the inward life. Some who are well versed in Eastern devotional works, which depict the Way of discipleship in colorful language and with a nomenclature which is far more abstract than applicable in character to the Western mind, may on first sight doubt this statement. I ask them to accept the challenge of it and take this chapter into the hour of meditation in the attitude of Pascal.

There is no appeal from it to any tribunal here or in heaven. It is the life of the disciple in its true and highest estate. No matter what books we have read or shall read, the challenge of the Cross stands before every disciple as a fact to be met, and not one can escape it. He may chart the Path to his mind's content, divide and subdivide it into discipleship, major and minor, occultist by virtue of this, mystic by virtue of that, near to the Master or far from him—the word of à Kempis is a two-edged sword which flashes clean to the heart of the problem of Initiation into Christ. The Cross of Christ descends bodily upon every soul of man who is resolved upon that Initiation. It is of no use for us, if as yet untried, to turn aside from this aspect of the Path because we may think it unduly introspective, if not morbid, in presentation. I can imagine that some, the academically and occultly learned ones, may feel inclined to do so, but that will not dispose of the fact.

If ever the Cross has been laid upon humanity, it has in this century above all others, nor could all the voices and commotion of the world hide the fact, whether it is recognized as the Cross of Christ or merely worldly misfortune is another matter. But it will make all the difference how we regard it, whether we recognize it as a stroke of common fate or see it as a major opportunity of the Cross, laid upon man for his own perfecting. To view it as a chance stroke of destiny will not carry us far. It may deaden the pain like a narcotic, leave us subdued and unresponsive, bound hand and foot to the relentless revolving wheel of time, uninspired and of no inspiration to our fellowmen. That has happened in countless lives. If it happened in all, we should not have to wait long for the downfall of civilization. Hence, the other view is imperative, that we face a turning point in evolution where men have been brought to an important crisis in life which offers an acceptance or rejection of a peculiar Initiation, by force, instead of by slow and easy development.

Between the two wars, mankind was settling down once again to humdrum, uneventful living, uneventful in higher and spiritual living, very eventful in seizing upon and making more and more of a materialistic environment and less and less susceptible to a frame of mind which turned back in quietness and continence to the perennial spring of spiritual inspiration and culture such as we find in *The Imitation*. And, looking back over the years and making an impartial assessment of our profit and loss, where do we find ourselves? What have we gained and what lost? I speak of mankind in general. The world crisis—and it is not yet ended— stripped mankind of most of its material gain, yet that has not taught it much. It may elect to build again in the same way upon the same foundations. The majority will do so, for they see nothing better, but this will not satisfy all. There are those, a comparatively small minority, who interpret the world crisis as a crisis in the soul of man, and through this crisis in these lives, Christ, it seems to me, will come into His own.

It has been said that purity of heart is to will one thing. That most pertinently sums up *The Imitation* and its author. Throughout the book, one thing only is willed. There is a single endeavor to mirror in the heart of men the image and life of Christ in all its radiant, poignant, and unrivaled beauty. There is not a word of deviation from this august ideal. It is as if the author had ever before him, day and night, the real presence of Christ in the Temple of the Heart, and not for a moment could he release his gaze from a rapt contemplation of it nor speak but in words of fervent simplicity of the way to full possession of it.

Acquainted as many of us are with many books of a devotional nature, when we turn to *The Imitation* and after repeated reflection upon it, it is astonishing to note how completely absorbed the author was in his subject. There is not a single aspect of the conduct of man, in his approach to or retrogression from the Christ ideal, which has escaped the clear insight of this genius of holiness.

In spite of some touches of austere asceticism, which we should expect from the pen of a recluse in monastic retirement, we find in him a warmth, companionship, and sympathetic understanding for man in all his manifold failings and weaknesses on the Way which places it in sharp contrast to the Eastern literature. How often does the complacent aloofness, conscious height of attainment, the bleak detachment so characteristic of the latter, seem to ignore or belittle our common and wounded humanity fighting at odds in a purely worldly environment and impress us with a feeling of finality and impossibility of achieving the high goal of endeavor while man is but man? Not so is it in *The Imitation*. The irresistible magnetism of Christ works upon the mind like a spiritual leaven as we read it.

It was the magnetism of Christ which gripped à Kempis as he wrote it, and it is this same influence which holds and compels our allegiance as we meditate it. Spiritual magnetism in an inspired writer has this of divinity in it: that it draws upward to itself, directly the heart is touched by it, and, as à Kempis depicts upon his living canvas in full and luminous colors the character of the Great Exemplar, we see a man lifted up into the high heaven of consciousness by the magnetism of his subject and writing what he must in perfect humility and consuming adoration.

Today our ears are deafened with the rhetoric of a thousand tongues. They are not inquisitorial tongues arraigning Christ. They have forgotten Him and arraign one another. There is a mad haste to build quickly upon the old foundations: power, prestige, and domination. Therefore is the name of it called Babel. For really, a few short years after the bloodbath of the nations, the fear of man for the ascendancy and domination of his neighbor rises steadily and makes the future as uncertain as the past. It is not a picture that would inspire any man. Whence then shall we look for inspiration and what shall we do?

We, who have striven through the years for the greater and enduring values of life and others like us of stiffer persuasions, are but a handful among the nations, but nothing that has happened has robbed us of our ideal or our hope. They are a part of the texture of soul which neither wars nor the rumor of wars can touch. Indeed, we are far more convinced than ever that these values are the only enduring ones, for after the world holocausts, they dominate the heart with an abated persistency, as silent witnesses of the presence of Christ within us. It is upon this foundation that we must continue to build.

We are not responsible for the masquerades of the nations nor did we create the gods they worship. "All gods of the nations are idols," says the Psalmist. That is a summary judgment, but in this materialistic epoch in which we find ourselves, is it not short of the truth? In fact, when we turn from it for a moment to quiet contemplation of *The Imitation,* we wonder whether after all à Kempis is speaking to humanity as we know it and whether it is fit to read it. We need it desperately, but the gods of the nations are firm upon their thrones. Two wars have not shaken them from their morbid seats, and it is humanity, our fellow men and women, who have kept them there. That is the unpalatable truth, but there is no gainsaying it. Christ has been dethroned by the people of the nations and as summarily dismissed as the grand inquisitor dismissed Him with a contemptuous finger pointing Him to the door.

À Kempis asks us to look at Christ, to meditate upon the beauty, suffering, and strength of Christ, and to realize that whatever happens to us as we try to radiate the influence of that life, we shall find the prototype of it in Him. There is our inspiration, and our care must be that we reflect it in a life of devoted service to the only ideal which is worth anything in this world.

ROSICRUCIAN CODE NO. 10

Lecture delivered 1968

The Rosicrucian's Code of Life set out in our Manual is no doubt familiar to us all. Yet my experience is that one can be so familiar with rules of this nature that their real inward significance is often overlooked and forgotten in regard to the application of them. These rules of the Code can easily share this fate. They can take their place among many others that are called platitudes and so bear little fruition in our lives. As a matter of fact, a whole volume of Rosicrucian instruction could be written on this Code and be a stimulating commentary of esoteric direction and behavior. Some of these rules are more penetrating in character than others. I am thinking particularly at the moment of Rule No. 10.* It is often in my mind.

> *Attempt no direct reforms in the lives of others. Discover in yourself what needs correction and improve yourself, that by the Light of your Life you may point the way to others.*

I sometimes think that we who are on the Path are apt to see the faults of others more quickly than other people by reason of our studies. I sometimes think we are more prone to attempt the reform of others than the keen, practical, hard-headed professional and business types we meet in the city, immersed in the affairs and struggles of daily contact, exercise toward their fellowmen. They usually see more truly the basic qualities of character and are more tolerant of the varied behavior, the personal reactions of their fellows, than we who assess them from what we consider the higher point of view.

---

*Note: In certain editions of the Manual this is listed as No. 9.

Why is this? Is it because, through the kindness of good Karma, we have been privileged to renew links from the past with those who are devoting themselves to esoteric development and are enjoying happy associations and therefore feel themselves much in advance of the majority—in this respect, who take no thought for the inner life? If this is not the basic cause, it is certainly one of the dangers of the Path. It has often been called the heresy of separateness. Yet it should scarcely occur to us to set down a demarcation line between ourselves and others who have not taken any thought for the Path. We do not know the potentialities of any human being and what may lie quiescent behind an unassuming exterior we know well. We should never assess people at their face value. If we do, we should be mistaken. Beyond the veil of personality lies the unsounded history of past lives, and if that history were suddenly revealed to us we should be astonished and humbled.

Regarding this rule, it is our first and paramount business to labor assiduously to know ourselves. There can be no end to that task. It is one of continuous work and reflection, trial and experience. If we believe that because we have read a number of books on the teaching of the Path and pass through certain grades of instruction we have the key to selfhood and other lives, experience will catch up with us and teach us better. Our grades, enlightening all along their varied course, are constantly a preparation, an instrumental technique, revealing a way of advancement to a point where we have to apply all we know to meet the experiences and eventualities of life wisely and well. But the revelation of self and its great possibilities lies beyond that and is subject to the conditions of the Karma of the past and cannot be foreseen or unduly hastened. If we know this is so with those who have taken thought for the Path and are treading it, surely it should incline us to feel charitably towards those who cooperate with us and those who do not—for life, in either case, is a hard school.

Now, speaking of ourselves who are engaged in this work, there is a factor which cannot be overlooked. It does not justify us in acting other than this rule enjoins, but it does reveal a reason why many on the Path do act in opposition to its teaching and often go out of their way to bluntly and untactfully attempt to reform others. Those who have been working upon themselves for some time esoterically are bound to feel the effects of that practice. The phlegmatic English for instance, with their native reserve and restraint, are more introverted than extroverted, but under the influence of higher training the temperament is liable to undergo considerable change. Etheric stimulation quickens, releases, and extends the vibrational range of contacts with others. Mental actions are prone to be swifter and therefore sometimes intolerant. The consequence is that what does not immediately harmonize in others with our own views is matter for criticism and an attempt to compel them to an alignment with our own thinking. I am sure that is often done with the best intentions. It seems to be a matter of personal duty, yet our real duty is to suggest, not to urge or compel. Reformation rarely comes on those terms. Others have to grow in their own way as we have, and they should be allowed their own conclusions and testing by experience.

The condition is somewhat similar to what happens to young students passing through school to the university. The strong stimulation of university life is more than they can comfortably adjust to, and some time has to elapse before they become assimilated to the new climate of thought and can do justice to themselves. As to discovering what needs correction in ourselves, if we are making headway in our studies, we should be fully conscious of our own shortcomings. We have long since been acquainted with the needful qualifications for advancement, because we have constantly in mind the lives of those who have been shining examples in the mystical life, and it is the latter part of the rule which claims our special attention " . . . that by the Light of your Life you may point the way."

If there is anything we should devoutly pray for, it is that we be given more Light. It is amazing to realize what mistakes we can make through the want of even a little more Light upon ourselves. Yet, we must learn to wait for it; we cannot force issues. All the Light we need, all the guidance we wait for, are present in the higher reaches of consciousness, and only through meditation and experience do we become gradually aligned to receive it. That pertains to our own private life, but our life in the world and in active service ever involves the lives of others, and that is where our chief problem lies: to throw the Light we have upon *them* and understand them.

One cannot go further in this theme without reverting to the thought of impersonality. It will readily be perceived why this is so, for if the insistent claims and concerns of the personal self unceasingly hold the field of attention, there is little hope of penetrating into and understanding the lives of others. At stated times, it is necessary to vacate the field, so to speak, and still the mental and emotional life and endeavor to rid us of the content and status of another self with whom we are dealing and wish to help. It is an exercise of psychometric art, and results will soon be noticed when once we have learned to be inwardly still, impersonal, and receptive to incoming impressions.

The great hindrance to success in this is that the conscious field is usually crowded with the conditions, happenings, and impressions of our own physical, emotional, and mental selves. There is no opportunity for the prevailing conditions in another self to be reflected in the mirror of consciousness. We cannot really understand others in this way, for the Light of the soul, which alone can rightly interpret, is not permitted to shine through us and reveal in others what we need to know to help them. To be still and silence the many voices of the personal self is the only sure way in which the many voices of other lives can be heard by us and known.

We are not without instruction to assist us in this, in our grades of teaching. Many have had considerable success in this art through the following of such instruction. The ideal, of course, is to be able to register the prevailing conditions of another life at long range in the absence of the person. I have known this to be done so effectively as to register very accurately the present physical condition, the tone of the emotional life, and the mental caliber of the person, its fullness and efficiency or otherwise and the degree of spiritual responsiveness. This kind of diagnosis may be a comparatively rare attainment, but it can be attempted. Its success would give one the real key to the most helpful service, but the basic requisite is a high degree of selflessness!

It will be noted how that basic qualification leads us back to the first part of the Rule we are considering on attempting direct reformation in other lives. Having that qualification, we should have no desire to do so. We shall be conscious of an inhibition against it. It is an interesting fact that, when we have passed certain crises of the Path, we reach a point in inner development when our attitude towards others undergoes a great change. Certain former insistent reactions of the personality fall away. We seem to be as removed from them. They do not urge us into action as hitherto. Where there was agitation, now there is peace. It is the goal for every aspirant too, and we are willing to let them find their own way with such assistance as they may ask and we can give them. We shall no longer demand that they be and do what we wish, but which they are not yet qualified esoterically to be and do. Our only wish will be to let such Light, as we ourselves have, fall upon them. The kindly and effective radiation of our own Light will prove ultimately the best gift we can make in the way of master service.

An ancient Greek philosopher said that all higher education of the intellect depends on cultivating our ability to understand one another. At first sight that does not appear to be a profound statement, yet its meaning underlies the very rule we are thinking of. We have only to substitute for the higher education of the intellect, the higher or soul consciousness in man. But, why should stress be put upon the ability to understand one another, as if *this* was of greatest importance, as if to see ourselves as we are and others as they are were a goal of great attainment? It is because our failure in these two directions lies at the root of all our differences, perplexities, and maladjustments in life, for the real man is invisible to ordinary sight and to the speculative intellect. He only becomes visible through the illumined mind, by our ascension of consciousness, our rising above the rationalistic intellect, by what the Greek calls "the higher education of the intellect." And the first stages of that process are included in the sensing of impressions in the way I have mentioned, by inward or upward direction and silence—and the sensing in service of others is the surest way of rising above the hampering veil of personality which obstructs knowledge and understanding of invisible selves.

However, the idea of service, which is the central feature of the Rosicrucian ideal, requires to be placed in a commonsense perspective. Some have rather a distorted view of the idea of helping others. They can waste valuable time which they need to help themselves, and they can relieve others of the necessary responsibility of standing upon their feet and seeking for themselves. We can and should help another to bear a difficult phase of Karma, which is very different from inviting others to place their karmic responsibilities upon ourselves. There are many even on the Path who seek to do this, because they are aware of the compassion and sympathy of the true server.

I believe the Masters help aspirants in their individual trials far more than they are conscious of, but that they do not and cannot liquidate the Karma which is theirs. The aspirant's whole development is conditioned by a karmic pattern, and he himself must so study himself and his life as to be able to meet it. But the burden of it, if it happens to be a burden, is within the knowledge of the

Masters to whom he aspires, and it is our duty in their name to help him to accept it and lighten it for him.

Perhaps the greatest sorrow of our time, and peculiarly incident to our time, is the individual and racial Karma which people have to bear, whether they are aspirants or not, and to relieve some of the keen pressure of it—nothing is so necessary and urgent as a deep understanding of self. Every step in that direction reveals to us more and more the fears, difficulties, and anxieties as well as the possibilities of those who are brought within our sphere of contact.

THE ROSICRUCIAN ORDER
Purpose and Work of the Order

Anticipating questions which may be asked by the readers of this book, the publishers take this opportunity to explain the purpose of the Order and how you may learn more about it.

There is only one universal Rosicrucian Order existing in the world today, united in its various jurisdictions, and having one Supreme Council in accordance with the original plan of the ancient Rosicrucian manifestoes. The Rosicrucian Order is not a religious or sectarian society.

This international organization retains the ancient traditions, teachings, principles, and practical helpfulness of the Order as founded centuries ago. It is known as the *Ancient Mystical Order Rosae Crucis,* which name, for popular use, is abbreviated into AMORC. The headquarters of the English Grand Lodge, AMORC, is located at San Jose, California.

The Order is primarily a humanitarian movement, making for greater health, happiness, and peace in people's *earthly lives,* for we are not concerned with any doctrine devoted to the interests of individuals living in an unknown, future state. The Work of Rosicrucians is to be done *here* and *now*; not that we have neither hope nor expectation of *another* life after this, but we *know* that the happiness of the future depends upon *what we do today for others* as well as for ourselves.

Secondly, our purposes are to enable all people to live harmonious, productive lives, as Nature intended, enjoying *all* the privileges of Nature and all benefits and gifts equally with all of humanity; and to be *free* from the shackles of superstition, the limits of ignorance, and the sufferings of avoidable *Karma.*

The Work of the Order, using the word "work" in an official sense, consists of teaching, studying, and testing such laws of God and Nature as make our members Masters in the Holy Temple (the physical body), and Workers in the Divine Laboratory (Nature's domains). This is to enable our members to render *more efficient help* to those who do not know, and who need or require help and assistance.

Therefore, the Order is a school, a college, a fraternity, with a laboratory. The members are students and workers. The graduates are unselfish servants of God to humanity, efficiently educated, trained, and experienced, attuned with the mighty forces of the Cosmic or Divine Mind, and Masters of matter, space, and time. This makes them essentially Mystics, Adepts, and Magi—creators of their own destiny. There are no other benefits or rights. All members are pledged to give unselfish service, without other hope or expectation of remuneration than to evolve the Self and prepare for a *greater* Work.

The Rosicrucian Sanctum membership program offers a means of personal home study. Instructions are sent regularly in specially pre-pared weekly lectures and lessons, and contain a summary of the Rosicrucian principles with such a wealth of personal experiments, exercises, and tests as will make each member highly proficient in the attainment of certain degrees of mastership. These correspondence lessons and lectures comprise several Degrees. Each Degree has its own Initiation ritual, to be performed by the member at home in his or her private home sanctum. Such rituals are not the elaborate rituals used in the Lodge Temples, but are simple and of practical benefit to the student.

If you are interested in knowing more of the history and present-day helpful offerings of the Rosicrucians, you may receive a *free* copy of the introductory booklet entitled the *Mastery of Life* by calling our toll-free telephone number 1-800-88-AMORC, or by writing to:

Rosicrucian Order, AMORC
1342 Naglee Avenue
San Jose, California 95191, U.S.A.

ROSICRUCIAN LIBRARY

SELF MASTERY AND FATE WITH THE CYCLES OF LIFE
by H. Spencer Lewis, Ph.D., F.R.C.

This book demonstrates how to harmonize the self with the cyclic forces of each life.

Happiness, health, and prosperity are available for those who know the periods in their own life that enhance the success of varying activities. Eliminate "chance" and "luck," cast aside "fate," and replace these with self mastery. Complete with diagrams and lists of cycles.

THE MYSTICAL LIFE OF JESUS
by H. Spencer Lewis, Ph.D., F.R.C.

A full account of Jesus' life, containing the story of his activities in the periods not mentioned in the Gospel accounts, *reveals the real Jesus* at last.

This book required a visit to Palestine and Egypt to secure verification of the strange facts found in Rosicrucian records. Its revelations, predating the discovery of the Dead Sea Scrolls, show aspects of the Essenes unavailable elsewhere.

This volume contains many mystical symbols (fully explained), photographs, and an unusual portrait of Jesus.

COSMIC MISSION FULFILLED
by Ralph M. Lewis, F.R.C.

This illustrated biography of Harvey Spencer Lewis, Imperator of the Ancient Mystical Order Rosae Crucis, was written in response to many requests from Rosicrucians and others who sought the key to this mystic-philosopher's life mission of rekindling the ancient flame of *Wisdom* in the Western world. We view his triumphs and tribulations from the viewpoint of those who knew him best.

Recognize, like him, that the present is our *moment in Eternity*; in it we fulfill our mission.

MANSIONS OF THE SOUL
by H. Spencer Lewis, Ph.D., F.R.C.

Reincarnation—the world's most disputed doctrine! What did Jesus mean when he referred to the "mansions in my Father's house"?

This book demonstrates what Jesus and his immediate followers knew about the rebirth of the soul, as well as what has been taught by sacred works and scholarly authorities in all parts of the world.

Learn about the cycles of the soul's reincarnations and how you can become acquainted with your present self and your past lives.

SECRET SYMBOLS OF THE ROSICRUCIANS
of the 16th and 17th Centuries

This large book is a rare collection of full-size plates of original Rosicrucian symbols and documents. A cherished possession for students of mysticism, this collection includes the Hermetic, alchemical, and spiritual meaning of the unique Rosicrucian symbols and philosophical principles passed down through the ages.

The plates are from originals and are rich in detail. The book is 12" by 18" and is bound in durable textured cover stock.

ROSICRUCIAN PRINCIPLES FOR THE HOME AND BUSINESS
by H. Spencer Lewis, Ph.D., F.R.C.

This volume contains the practical application of Rosicrucian teachings to such problems as: ill health, common ailments, how to increase one's income or promote business propositions. It shows not only what to do, but what to avoid, in using metaphysical and mystical principles in starting and bringing into realization new plans and ideas.

Both business organizations and business authorities have endorsed this book.

GREAT WOMEN INITIATES or the Feminine Mystic
by Hélène Bernard, F.R.C.

Throughout history, there have been women of exceptional courage and inspiration. Some, such as Joan of Arc, are well known; others have remained in relative obscurity—until now. In this book, Hélène Bernard examines from a Rosicrucian viewpoint the lives of thirteen great women mystics. Her research and insight have unveiled these unsung heroines who, even in the face of great adversity, have staunchly defended freedom of thought and the light of mysticism.

THE MYSTIC PATH
by Raymund Andrea, F.R.C.

This informative and inspirational work will guide you across the threshold of mystical initiation. The author provides insights into the states of consciousness and experiences you may have as you travel the Mystic Path. It is filled with the fire and paths of the initiate's quest. His spiritual, mental, and physical crises are fully described and pondered. Andrea's deep understanding of the essence of Western mystical and transcendental thought makes this a book you will treasure and refer to often as you advance in your mystical studies. Among the many topics addressed are: Meditation, Contemplation, Awakening Consciousness, the Dark Night of the Soul, Mystical Participation, and Mystical Union.

"UNTO THEE I GRANT . . ."
as revised by Sri Ramatherio

Out of the mysteries of the past comes this antique book that was written two thousand years ago, but was hidden in manuscript form from the eyes of the world and given only to the Initiates of the temples in Tibet to study privately.

It can be compared only with the writings attributed to Solomon in the Bible of today. It deals with human passions, weaknesses, fortitudes, and hopes. Included is the story of the expedition into Tibet that secured the manuscript and the Grand Lama's permission to translate it.

THE TECHNIQUE OF THE DISCIPLE
by Raymund Andrea, F.R.C.

The Technique of the Disciple contains a modern description of the ancient esoteric path to spiritual Illumination, trod by the masters and avatars of yore. It has long been said that Christ left, as a great heritage to members of his secret council, a private method for guidance in life, which method has been preserved until today in the secret mystery schools.

The author reveals the method for attaining a greater life taught in these mystery schools, which perhaps parallels the secret instructions of Christ to members of his council. The book is informative, inspiring, and splendidly written.

THE TECHNIQUE OF THE MASTER
or The Way of Cosmic Preparation
by Raymund Andrea, F.R.C.

A guide to inner unfoldment! The newest and simplest explanation for attaining the state of Cosmic Consciousness. To those who have felt the throb of a vital power within, and whose inner vision has at times glimpsed infinite peace and happiness, this book is offered. It converts the intangible whispers of self into forceful actions that bring real joys and accomplishments in life. It is a masterful work on psychic unfoldment.

WHISPERINGS OF SELF
by Validivar

Wisdom, wit, and insight combine in these brief aphorisms that derive from the interpretation of cosmic impulses received by Validivar, whose true name was Ralph M. Lewis, former Imperator of the Rosicrucian Order.

These viewpoints of all areas of human experience make an attractive gift as well as a treasured possession of your own.

THE SYMBOLIC PROPHECY OF
THE GREAT PYRAMID
by H. Spencer Lewis, Ph.D., F.R.C.

The world's greatest mystery and first wonder is the Great Pyramid. Its history, vast wisdom, and prophecies are all revealed in this beautifully bound and illustrated book. You will be amazed at the pyramid's scientific construction and at the secret knowledge of its mysterious builders.

THE SANCTUARY OF SELF
by Ralph M. Lewis, F.R.C.

Are you living your life to your best advantage? Are you beset by a *conflict of desires?* Do you know that there are various *loves* and that some of them are dangerous drives?

Learn which of your feelings to discard as enslaving influences and which to retain as worthy incentives.

The author brings to you from his years of experience, the practical aspects of mysticism.

MENTAL POISONING
Thoughts That Enslave Minds
by H. Spencer Lewis, Ph.D., F.R.C.

Must humanity remain at the mercy of evil influences created in the minds of the vicious? Do poisoned thoughts find innocent victims? Use the knowledge this book fearlessly presents as an antidote for such superstitions and their influences.

There is no need to remain helpless even though evil thoughts of envy, hate, and jealousy are aimed to destroy your self-confidence and peace of mind.

THE UNIVERSE OF NUMBERS

From antiquity, the strangest of systems attempting to reveal the universe has been that of numbers. This book goes back to the mystical meaning and inherent virtue of numbers. It discusses the Qabalistic writings contained in the *Sepher Yezirah,* and correlates the teachings of Pythagoras, Plato, Hermes Trismegistus, Philo, Plotinus, Boehme, Bacon, Fludd, and others who have explored this fascinating subject.

MENTAL ALCHEMY
by Ralph M. Lewis, F.R.C.

We can transmute our problems to workable solutions through *mental alchemy.* While this process is neither easy nor instantaneously effective, eventually the serious person will be rewarded. Certain aspects of our lives *can* be altered to make them more compatible with our goals.

Use this book to alter the direction of your life through proper thought and an understanding of practical mystical philosophy.

MYSTICS AT PRAYER
Compiled by Many Cihlar, F.R.C.

The first compilation of the famous prayers of the renowned mystics and adepts of all ages.

The book *Mystics at Prayer* explains in simple language the reason for prayer, how to pray, and the cosmic laws involved. You learn the real efficacy of prayer and its full beauty dawns upon you. Whatever your religious beliefs, this book makes your prayers the application not of words, but of helpful, divine principles. You will learn the infinite power of prayer. Prayer, your rightful heritage, is the direct means of communion with the infinite force of divinity.

MYSTICISM—THE ULTIMATE EXPERIENCE
by Cecil A. Poole, F.R.C.

An experience is more than just a sensation, a feeling. It is an awareness, or perception, with meaning. Our experiences are infinite in number, yet they are limited to certain types. Some are related to our objective senses; others, to dreams and inspirational ideas. But there is *one* that transcends them all—the *mystical experience*. It serves every category of our being: it stimulates, it enlightens; it is the *Ultimate Experience*.

And this book, *Mysticism—The Ultimate Experience*, defines it in simple and inspiring terms.

SON OF THE SUN
by Savitri Devi

The amazing story of Akhnaton (Amenhotep IV), Pharaoh of Egypt, 1360 B.C. This is not just the fascinating story of one life—it is far more. It raises the curtain on humanity's emerging from superstition and idolatry. Against the tremendous opposition of a fanatical priesthood, Akhnaton brought about the world's first spiritual revolution. He was the first to declare that there was a "sole God." In the words of Sir Flinders Petrie *(History of Egypt)*: "Were it invented to satisfy our modern scientific conceptions, his religio-philosophy could not be logically improved upon at the present day."

ORDER BOOKS FROM:

ALEXANDRIA CATALOG SALES
1-800-241-5422

Rosicrucian Order, AMORC
1342 Naglee Avenue
San Jose, California 95191, U.S.A.

For a complete, illustrated catalog and
price list of the books listed herein,
please call or write to the address listed above.